O God of peace, who hast taught us that in returning and
rest we shall be saved, in quietness and confidence shall be
our strength: By the might of thy Spirit lift us, we pray thee,
to thy presence, where we may be still and know that thou
art God; through Jesus Christ our Lord. Amen.
(BCP)

be
PRESENT

John MacMurray

Early in my career, I remember one of my first hikes to a small waterfall in the Columbia River Gorge. It was a moderate walk through beautiful forest only twenty or so minutes from my car. As I approached the waterfall the trail opened up into a little alcove of fir trees and lush green. Water was pouring from a gap in the rock about eighty feet above the path and descending into a crystal stream that cut its way through the maples and ferns along its banks. A gentle breeze from the mist caused the leaves to sway. It was beautifully quiet; only the voice of the water was allowed to speak. The trees stood majestically, encircling the waterfall like guardians protecting a wonderful treasure. A small bird landed on a branch a few feet away, officially welcoming me to this special place.

After a few photos, I sat in silence. I felt a peace and pleasure that was almost palpable. I wanted to stay. The tranquility of the landscape beckoned me to something more than rest or relaxation.

Why do we long for places like these? Could it be that we are wired in such a way as to perceive beauty in our natural world and then respond in appreciation for it? Certainly we all seek a measure of relief from our everyday stress. But it is more than that. What

I experienced at the waterfall is what I would call *presence*. Free from the distractions of civilization, the waterfall became for me a sacred place.

It seems there is something wonderfully unique about the nature of human beings. We alone, from among all the creatures on this planet, view nature with an appreciation for its beauty. We are interested in nature not only in a functional sense, as all other creatures are, but in an aesthetic sense as well. And this, as far as I can tell, is universal among the human species.

The feelings I experienced that day would have been essentially the same for anyone else who might have been in my place. We use words such as majestic, grandeur, splendor, awesome, and magnificent to describe the beauty of nature. So this begs the question, *Why is nature so beautiful to us?*

As a follower of Jesus, I come to this question with some assumptions. Here's one: Before the universe came to be, before the earth was brought forth in all its beauty and splendor, before human life was fashioned with grace and glory, before there was *anything*, there was the life of shared communion of the Father, Son, and Spirit. Every act of this God, every thought and every dream, has flowed from their shared life.

So, if the fundamental or deepest truth of God's being is his existence as the relationship of Father, Son, and Spirit, then the larger story of creation and even atonement is really about love, relationship, and sharing life. The natural world, then, is like a sacrament to remember the sheer beauty of their love expressed in everything they do. Creation becomes a never-ending open invitation to know God.

Consequently, I have come to believe the reverence and awe that I experience in the natural world is not simply for the things I see, as beautiful and wonderful as they are. It is ultimately for the God who made them. It is the Creator God that nature, in all of its splendor and magnificence, compellingly points us toward. ◧

To learn more about John and his photography visit: www.creationcalendars.com

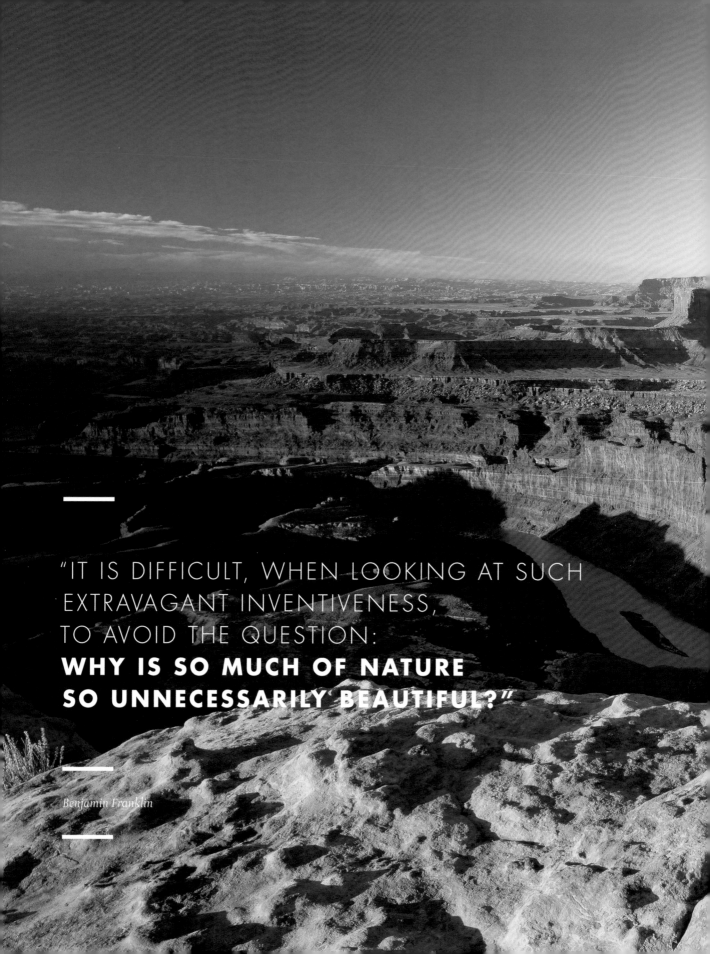

"IT IS DIFFICULT, WHEN LOOKING AT SUCH
EXTRAVAGANT INVENTIVENESS,
TO AVOID THE QUESTION:
**WHY IS SO MUCH OF NATURE
SO UNNECESSARILY BEAUTIFUL?"**

Benjamin Franklin

THE HEAVENS DECLARE THE GLORY OF GOD;
THE SKIES PROCLAIM THE WORK OF HIS HANDS.
DAY AFTER DAY THEY POUR FORTH SPEECH;
NIGHT AFTER NIGHT THEY DISPLAY KNOWLEDGE.
**THERE IS NO SPEECH OR LANGUAGE WHERE
THEIR VOICE IS NOT HEARD.**

Psalm 19: 1-3

THE CONTEMPLATION OF A BEAUTIFUL
LANDSCAPE EXCITES THE HIGHEST SPIRITUAL
PLEASURE IN US.

John Muir

EDITOR'S NOTE

Be present. It's a simple idea, easy to shrug off. But more than ever for a leader in the church to be and remain effective in their role, this two-word mantra is invaluable.

When our team gathered to think through this year's content in light of the theme, our minds wondered: What would it look like for this leadership review to act more like a leadership devotional? How could we present the content in a way that was fresh while expressing the idea of being present?

Our solution? Get rid of the noise. As you read through, you'll come upon an interview with Mark Batterson. We caught Mark just before he began a sabbatical. For Mark that meant heading out west to be astonished at God's grandeur. In the interview Mark emphasizes how important it is to get rid of the noise—to rid ourselves of the phones and emails and meetings and everything else pulling at our schedules—and get quiet before the Lord.

We took Mark's advice. You've already noticed that we've nixed the front matter including the table of contents. Don't worry, it's in the back if you get lost. We were intentional about aggregating longer pieces this year, articles and features that demand us to take time to read.

We were also intentional about providing opportunities for reflection and discussion along the way. The "Reflection" pages offer some insights and questions and also link to the Elements of the Catalyst Leader *(Passion for God, Community, Integrity, Influence, Engaging Culture, Courageous in Calling)*. You will also encounter additional discussion sections that we attached to pieces we thought cried out for it. So you can grab your favorite chair or assemble your small group and dive in.

You'll notice we deposited several prayer breaks throughout as well. Don't skip over these. Use the opportunity to read the prayer to the Lord. Our hope is that you slow down as you work through the magazine, thoughtfully engaging with all the content while seeking God's voice and prompting. What is He saying to you? How is He challenging you?

If this feels a bit liturgical to you that's okay. Imagine the thousands of other leaders who are reading through this and praying the same prayers. We're all lifting our voices to God in unison—a beautiful chorus of praise to God.

I'm writing this note to you in Bend, Oregon. I'm here on a writing retreat. Out the back door I can see Mt. Bachelor resting in the gold light of the setting sun. There's no television on, my email's turned off, and my phone is nowhere to be found, and I'm praying for you. I'm praying for your walk with Jesus. I'm lifting up your goals and dreams. I'm praying the Lord convicts you as you read through the pages before you. And I'm praying our efforts will encourage you to press into God like you never have before. I'm praying you find yourself on your face, surrendering that one thing you've been holding on to for so long, that thing keeping you from a fuller, more abundant life in Christ.

Now, Brook Fraser is playing on the stereo and the gold on Mt. Bachelor is nearly gone. "I will exalt you," she sings. The words dig deep into me, as I'm sure they do to you.

We can never be reminded enough to be present, in our work and ministries and families. But my heart's wish is that we all find the time to be present before our King. "Our treasure, Lord, You are."

Here we stand, Lord. Purify us. Here we kneel, Lord, we lift You up. Here we lay, our faces down. Wreck us, Lord. And do a mighty work.

To my brothers and sisters with deep love,

Tim

HERE WE STAND, LORD. PURIFY US. HERE WE KNEEL LORD, WE LIFT YOU UP. HERE WE LAY, OUR FACES DOWN. WRECK US, LORD. AND DO A MIGHTY WORK.

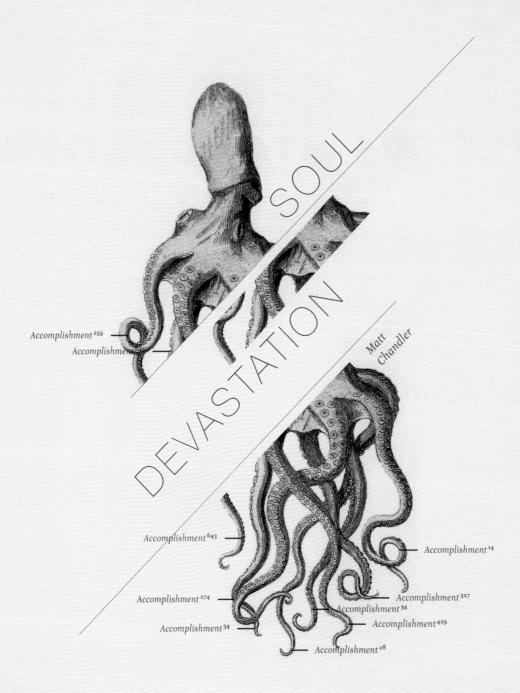

SOUL

DEVASTATION

Matt Chandler

Accomplishment [259]

Accomplishment

Accomplishment [643]

Accomplishment [14]

Accomplishment [274]

Accomplishment [327]

Accomplishment [34]

Accomplishment [34]

Accomplishment [429]

Accomplishment [28]

My concerns started on a Saturday night at a "Celebration Weekend" several years ago. Our church—The Village—was baptizing a great deal of men and women who were publicly professing their belief in Jesus Christ as their Lord and Savior. As I walked into our small auditorium I was greeted by a hefty man in his early 20s.

He gave me a hug and then told me about a girl he had brought to hear the testimonies. With a bit of nervous glee in his voice he informed me that the girl was a witch, and he hadn't told her ahead of time where he was bringing her. With a smile on his face, he told me she was really angry and he wanted me to know this "just in case something happened."

I sat down on the front row and, with some anxiety, prayed that God would give me wisdom if this thing turned into a scene from Harry Potter: The Unrated Version.

About this time the screen obstructing the baptistry was raised, and standing in the water were two women in their early 30s. Karen[1] began to share her testimony. She told us for the last fifteen years of her life she had been heavily involved in the occult and witchcraft. She began to list all the reasons Christ was better, more

powerful and more loving than anything or anyone else, especially compared with what she had witnessed and been a part of in the occult.

I breathed a sigh of relief and knew God was at work among us. A young man in his early 20s was next. He talked of atheism, alcohol, Buddhism, drugs, and doubt, and then he talked about how through the patience and persistence of a friend, the Holy Spirit opened his eyes to the truth of life in Christ and forgiveness through his cross.

OUR NONCHALANT FAITH

But the next four baptisms bothered me. One after another, each person stirred the waters and told some variation of the same story:

"I grew up in church. We went every Sunday morning and night. We even went to Wednesday prayer, Vacation Bible School, and youth camp. If the doors were open, we were there.

"I was baptized when I was six, seven, or eight, but didn't understand what the gospel was, and after a while I lost interest in church and Jesus, and I started walking in open sin. Someone recently sat me down and explained it, or invited me to The Village and I heard the gospel for the first time.

"I was blown away. How did I miss that?" Or they would say, "No one ever taught me that."

I had heard all this before but that night was the eve of the birth of our son Reid. My daughter was three and it hit me that my kids were going to grow up in the church. That night, for the first time, I asked the question, "How can you grow up going to church every week and *not* hear the gospel?" I quickly decided that these people had heard the gospel but didn't have the spiritual ears to *truly* hear it, to receive it.

Fortunately, the Holy Spirit wasn't going to let it go that easily. The question began to haunt me. I decided to have a few conversations and interviews with what we have called the "de-churched" men and women attending The Village. A few of them confirmed my hunch was correct. They could go back and read journals and sermon notes from when they were teenagers or college students and see that they had indeed heard the gospel.

What alarmed me most, however, was the number of men and women who couldn't do that. Their old journals and student Bibles were filled with what Christian Smith in his excellent book *Soul Searching* called "Christian Moralistic Therapeutic Deism."[2] This mode of thinking is religious, even "Christian" in its content, but more about self-actualization and self-fulfillment, positing a God who does not so much intervene and redeem but basically hangs out behind the scenes, cheering on your you-ness and hoping you pick up the clues he's left to become the best you you can be.

The Moralistic Therapeutic Deism passing for Christianity in many of the churches these young adults grew up in includes talk about Jesus and about being good and avoiding bad—especially about feeling good about one's self—and God factored into all of that, but the gospel message simply wasn't there.

What I found was that for a great deal of young twenty-somethings and thirty-somethings, the gospel had been merely *assumed*, not taught or proclaimed as central. No one made it explicit to them.

NOTHING NEW

This assumption has historical precedent. We can read about it in the pages of Scripture and in the chronicles of church history. Consider these words from Paul in 1 Corinthians 15:1-5a (ESV):

Now I would remind you, brothers, of the gospel I preached to you, which you received, in which you stand, and by which you are being saved, if you hold fast to the word I preached to you—unless you believed in vain.

For, I delivered to you as of first importance what I also received: that Christ died for our sins in accordance with the Scriptures, that he was buried, that he was raised on the third day in accordance with the Scriptures.

Paul is reminding the Christians of the gospel. He's saying, "Don't forget it! You were saved by it, will be sustained by it, and are currently standing in it."

For some reason—namely, our depravity—we have a tendency to think that the cross saves us from past sin and now we have to take over and clean ourselves up. This sort of thinking is devastating to the soul. The assumed gospel occurs when well-meaning teachers, leaders, and preachers set out to see lives first and foremost conformed to a pattern of behavior (religion) and not transformed by the Holy Spirit's power (gospel).

The Apostle Paul saw this bad teaching and practice happen often, and he went on the offensive against it:

I am astonished that you are so quickly deserting him who called you in the grace of Christ and are turning to a different gospel—not that there is another one, but there are some who trouble you and want to distort the gospel of Christ. But even if we or an angel from heaven should preach to you a gospel contrary to the one we preached to you, let him be accursed.

IN [PHILIPPIANS 3:4-9] PAUL STATES THAT ALL HIS RELIGIOUS EFFORT, **EXHAUSTIVE CHECKLIST OF ALL HIS ACCOMPLISHMENTS INCLUDED**, AMOUNTED TO NOTHING COMPARED TO THE SURPASSING GREATNESS OF CHRIST.

As we have said before, so now I say again: If anyone is preaching to you a gospel contrary to the one you received, let him be accursed.
(Galatians 1:6-9 ESV).

I have been crucified with Christ. It is no longer I who live, but Christ who lives in me. And the life I now live in the flesh I live by faith in the Son of God, who loved me and gave himself for me. I do not nullify the grace of God, for if righteousness were through the law, then Christ died for no purpose.

O foolish Galatians! Who has bewitched you? It was before your eyes that Jesus Christ was publicly portrayed as crucified. Let me ask you only this: Did you receive the Spirit by works of the law or by hearing with faith? Are you so foolish? Having begun by the Spirit, are you now being perfected by the flesh? Did you suffer so many things in vain—if indeed it was in vain? Does he who supplies the Spirit to you and works miracles among you do so by works of the law, or by hearing with faith … ?
(Galatians 2:20 - 3:5 ESV).

The idolatry that exists in man's heart always wants to lead him away from his Savior and back to his own self-reliance no matter how pitiful that self-reliance is or how many times it has betrayed him. Religion is usually the tool the self-righteous man uses to exalt himself.

Again this isn't new; in Philippians 3:4-9, the Apostle Paul lays out his religious pedigree and practice as an example of what a man can accomplish with discipline and hard work. In that passage Paul states that all his religious effort, exhaustive checklist of all his accomplishments included, amounted to nothing compared to the surpassing greatness of Christ. He goes a step further and even calls it "rubbish" or "dung."

Think about that: all your church attendance, all your religious activities, your Sunday School attendance medals, your journals, having a "quiet time," reading the Scriptures … it's all in vain if you don't have Christ. When you read these texts together you get a feel for Paul's attack on the "Christian Moralistic Therapeutic Deism" of his day.

We are saved, sanctified, and sustained by what Jesus did for us on the cross and through the power of his resurrection. If you add to or subtract from the cross, even if it is to factor in biblically-mandated religious practices like prayer and evangelism, you rob God of his glory and Christ of his sufficiency. **C**

---

[1] Not her real name.

[2] Christian Smith with Melinda Lundquist Denton, *Soul Searching: The Religious and Spiritual Lives of American Teenagers* (Oxford University Press, 2009), 118.

KOLKATA, INDIA

FOLLOW ME

Jonathan Merritt

The Kolkata sun was just peaking over the horizon when I awoke. I'd been in India for a little more than four days but my body was resisting the time change. Rolling onto my back, I stared into the barely visible ceiling of my room at the YMCA.

Paint peeling.

Muggy.

Mosquitoes.

Circling my head, one pest finally landed on my cheek and pricked my skin; my reticence to move almost convinced me to let him finish his breakfast. I begrudgingly swatted into the air, and as my insect wake-up call flew away, I rose to begin my day.

I had been traveling with my friend Chris Heuertz, executive director of Word Made Flesh (WMF). The mission of WMF is "Serving Jesus Among the Poorest of the Poor." From building orphanages for children with AIDS to rescuing women from the sex trade to ministering to people who are poor in South America's most destitute favellas, WMF pursues their mission in places that would make most American Christians cringe.

Our seventeen-day trek would land us in two Indian states as well as Kathmandu, Nepal and Bangkok, Thailand. This day, we were in Kolkata where Chris had arranged for me to serve in one of Mother Teresa's homes for the infirmed and dying.

On this particular day, I rose just after six to begin getting ready for my work. Due to water rationing, I was unable to take a shower—an inconvenience I came to realize was normative for many Indians. Luckily, I filled two buckets with water before going to bed the night before. Stripping off my clothes, I squatted on a concrete floor to pour the frigid water over my naked body. Alongside the water, my thoughts also washed over me, and I wondered what the ongoing work of the inevitable "Saint Teresa" would be like.

A WMF field director soon arrived, and we sped through the congested, polluted city of more than fifteen million. Arriving at the Missionaries of Charity convent around seven, I stopped by Mother Teresa's grave for a moment to pay my respects. Her simple white stone grave aligned her death with her life—no extravagance, no decoration. After a few moments of quiet, I left to meet Sister Mercy who registered me for service and sent me on my way.

A short bus ride later, I turned up at a massive facility in the middle of a dilapidated slum. The trash and begging poor created a gauntlet of obstacles in route to the entrance. A sign atop the building read, "Premdan," meaning "house of love."

As we entered, we were not greeted by anyone—no volunteer coordinator, no facility manager. No, there was too much important work to do. I froze, overwhelmed and unsure about where to begin. I walked over to the male ward where volunteers scurried between patients, bandaging their wounds, shaving their faces, and cutting their hair. This is what I think the Pool of Bethesda must have been like as I wandered through a hoard of males, most of them lying on the ground in the courtyard, quietly looking into the distance.

I couldn't imagine the shame these men must have felt; I coveted their thoughts.

My feet led me up the stairs of the men's housing unit, and the conditions surprisingly worsened. Beds were laid out on a grid throughout the expansive room. Emaciated bodies lay upon the sheets, and moans filled the air. I could only imagine that the aches of their illnesses worsened in the isolation of their pain. I stood motionless for several minutes. Contemplating. Processing.

"You sir," a man said clasping my shoulder. "Come assist me."

From his accent, it was clear that the man was German. The ripples on his sun-scorched cheeks led me to believe he was about eighty years old. Following him, I approached a patient lying next to the door whose foot was swollen to three or four times the normal size. The skin's green hue told me it was probably gangrenous.

"He hasn't bathed in more than ten years," the German informed me. "The skin around his wound is like the scales of a fish and must be scrubbed before we can treat him. It's going to be very painful, and I'll need to hold him down."

He reached into his pocket and handed me a wire brush like the one I clean my grill with.

"Scrub," he barked, grasping the man's shoulders and pressing him into the wall against which he was leaning.

"Scrub with all your strength!"

As soon as I began, the man started screaming. I pushed through his cries, continuing to scrub his foot. Dead skin accumulated on the tops of my sandal-strapped feet and made piles between my toes. His skin bled in places but the German continued to press me.

Despite my efforts to ignore them, the cries of the patient were impossible to block out.

"Please, Baba," the man begged me. "Please stop. Please."

"Baba" means father. The man thought I was a priest. Tears pooled in my eyes as I relentlessly scrubbed.

Finally, we finished and the German handed me a small jar of Vaseline and some toenail clippers.

"Now make him love you again," he said.

I rubbed the salve into the fresh skin on his leg before clipping his gnarled toenails. His breathing patterns returned to normal.

"Thank you, Baba," he said.

I turned to depart, already looking for a place to slip away and have a good cry, but the German bellowed from across the room.

"We have more work to do."

I rushed to his side where he was attending to a skeleton lying on his back. From what I could tell, every strand of muscle tissue on this man's bones was gone. Skin hung off his appendages like bat wings. His protruding hipbones looked like ball bearings.

We rubbed down the stick figure of a man with coconut oil and cream, being careful to mind the bedsores. The man groaned.

"Make him comfortable," the German instructed as he rose to walk away. "He will be gone before morning."

I continued to gently massage this man's body, lifting his sides to access his back. I stooped to pray in his ear as tears fell from my face to his pillow, but I knew not whether he could hear me. His jaw hung open and he stared into the air; his eyes were empty.

When I finished, I washed my hands and again joined the German, this time accepting my role as his assistant. No interview necessary—there was no time. For the next several hours we performed humiliating procedures and unspeakable tasks for the infirmed and dying.

Finally, a bell rang.

"It's time for tea," he said tossing his gloves into a rusty trashcan.

* * *

I took my time walking to the pavilion. Entering the open space, I took a plastic cup filled with black tea and milk and joined the German who was already resting under the shade of a tree. I felt like I needed to be alone, but this man had become my boss and my friend over the past several hours. The least I could do is engage him in some actual conversation.

His name was "Helmut," and he'd been coming to Premdan for ten years in six-month rotations. During this time, he had become something of a self-educated doctor, but in his pre-Kolkata days he'd been a Lutheran minister.

I was struggling to find something profound to ask this sage.

"Some great theologians have come from Germany over the years, huh?" I asked as a where-did-that-come-from look appeared across my face.

Helmut said he believed the best days of the German church were gone. Church leaders in Germany were struggling with an increasingly secular society. They started focusing energy on petitioning the government for institutional recognition. The church in Germany was so busy fighting with businesses and government trying to get everyone to recognize their existence and their preferences. But along the way, he said, they'd lost themselves and they've lost sight of their mission.

"I suppose the German church and the American church are not so different as one might think," Helmut said.

"I suppose not," I agreed.

He turned to me with a look that only an aged and experienced person can give. It was as if his eyes were prophesying, telling me to listen up because I was about to receive some great wisdom.

"Christians in America and Germany forget that it is not what you think or how much power you have or how you vote that changes the world. It's your hands that do the changing."

He wiggled his pruny digits.

"I held that man as you cleaned his feet. Did we change him? Perhaps. But he'll need to be cleaned again. I *do* know that he changed us," Helmut reflected. "In a small way, God worked through us and, as a result, this world moved just a touch closer to what he'd have it be.

"That's really why I'm here," he continued. "When I had my own congregation, I'd read Jesus' words in Matthew about being the salt of the earth, but I didn't fully understand it."

He turned to look out over the courtyard.

"Now I know."

I sat in silence, stunned by the way this man had summed up everything I'd been feeling. He'd seen the way the church had been led astray from her mission, seduced by power and lured by partisanship. Reconciling the teachings of Jesus with the actions of his church was difficult for him. He'd come to Mother Teresa's hospital confused and hungry, and there he found everything he'd been looking for—hope, inspiration, and answers.

Helmut looked down again at the gnarled hands in his lap, and the bell rang for work to begin again.

***

The experience is as fresh on my heart today as it was when it happened. I keep seeing Helmut's hands in my mind, and I keep thinking about Jesus. I find myself weighing the old man's words against the stories of the Gospels—from healings to feedings, from Christ's life to his death and resurrection—and I think he's onto something.

Jesus didn't begin his ministry with an outlined agenda. Instead, he launched his public work with two simple words: "Follow me." And then he set out on a living lecture to illustrate to us what following him looked like. He healed the sick and fed the hungry, he worked miracles that still boggle modern minds. He preached the kingdom, promoted a new way of living, and then bore his cross to a hill called the place of the skull where he offered his life as a sacrifice for all.

When religion squelches our childlike faith, we're driven back to Jesus' first words. When we feel alone in our spiritual journeys—those moments when we find ourselves staring into the stars and begging the Creator to speak to us—Jesus' words echo into our lives. "Follow me," our Savior says. "Press your feet into my footprints. Look at my life and walk the path I've carved out for you."

Jesus was always touching people, playing with children, and rubbing his spit in someone's eyes. He was present with those who needed him, never content to let his disciples do the work for him. If following Jesus means living like Christ did, then it must cost something.

Time.

Resources.

Vocation.

Even our lives.

Jesus' life was actually the key to Jesus' effectiveness. When he opened his mouth, he was a great teacher and his words melted the crowds. But there were countless good teachers in his day. What set Jesus a notch above them? The Scripture says that Christ left people slack-jawed "because he taught as one who had authority, and not as their teachers of the law." (Matthew 7:29 NIV)

What could Matthew possibly mean? Jesus may have been a rabbi, but he didn't have a synagogue. He was a teacher, but no school claimed him. The difference is that Jesus didn't just prophesy from on high, promoting a list of rules and claiming to care about "issues." Jesus embodied everything he taught.

WE MUST BE PRESENT AMONG THOSE WHO NEED US, GIVING OURSELVES TO THEM AND FOR THEM. JESUS' LIFE IS IN STARK CONTRAST TO MOST CULTURE WARRING CHRISTIANS. HE DIDN'T JUST ADVOCATE. **HE LIVED AND DWELLED AND TOUCHED AND HEALED.**

As Jesus-followers we can't flip through the browning pages of the Bible, reading about Jesus' life and then go do something else—vote or mobilize or advocate. We can't rely on others to do the work for us. We must be present among those who need us, giving ourselves to them and for them. Jesus' life is in stark contrast to most culture warring Christians. He didn't just advocate. He lived and dwelled and touched and healed.

The Apostle John was getting at this idea when he said, "This is how we know we are living in him. Those who say they live in God should live their lives as Jesus did." (I John 2:5-6 NLT).

John speaks a word for us today here by saying, "If you claim to love who Jesus is, you should walk like Jesus did." Today, two billion people on planet earth claim to follow Jesus, and I wonder how many of their lives look like his. Does yours? Does mine?

The formula for following Jesus is simple: Follow. Jesus. Walk like he walked, live like he lived, give yourself to others, and share the good news that God has brought freedom to us all. Being faithful disciples of Christ in this century is no different than it was two millennia ago. If that's what we claim to be, we must make good on our professions of faith.

Is it enough to "advocate" for the hungry when we can satiate their hunger? Can we claim to follow Jesus if we do nothing ourselves for the poor he cared so much about? And what of the plight of orphans and the abandoned elderly? Does God let us off the hook when we ignore their problems except every fourth week in November?

A hospital is filled to overflowing with the sick and dying in Kolkata, India. And in Russia. And China. And Nigeria. They are waiting for the good news of Jesus to be declared and embodied. And I have a feeling more than a few here in America—the broken, the abused, the outcast, the poor—need the same.

Like Helmut, may we engage our hands for Jesus through service and sacrifice for others. May we scrub the wounds of those who need it, realizing that it's often as painful for us as it is for them. May we press our feet into the steps Christ once trod, following him away from an "advocacy only" religion to a "follow me" faith. ▣

Jonathan Merritt is the author of *A Faith of Our Own* (April 2012). This article is excerpted from his book. Copyright Faithwords, a division of Hachette Book Group. Reprinted by permission.

PRAYER OF MOTHER TERESA

Dear Jesus, Help us to spread your fragrance every-
where we go, flood our souls with your Spirit and life.
Penetrate and possess our whole being so utterly that
our lives may only be a radiance of yours. Shine through
us and be so in us that every soul we come in contact
with may feel your presence in our soul. Let them look
up and see no longer us but only Jesus. Stay with us and
then we shall begin to shine as you shine, so to shine
as to be light to others. The light, O Jesus, will be all
from you. None of it will be ours. It will be your shining on others through us. Let us thus praise you in the
way you love best by shining on those around us. Let us
preach you without preaching not by words, but by our
example by the catching force the sympathetic influence of what we do the evident fullness of the love our
hearts bear to you.

RISKY
BUSINESS

>>>>>>>>>>>>>>>>>> **JUDAH SMITH**

Over the last two years, our church has faced some of the biggest challenges and adjustments in its nineteen-year history. Two of the most significant included a transition to new lead pastors and the passing of my dad, the founding pastor.

As you can imagine, a lot has changed in the church recently. But by the grace of God and with the help of many amazing leaders and friends, we have not lost momentum. If anything, we sense ourselves rallying. Greater things are yet to come; our best days are ahead.

In practical terms, this means more things are going to change! Life and growth require rethinking, pruning, reinventing, and stepping out. The future God has for our church—for all churches—implies a certain degree of risk. Just read the Great Commission. Mark 16:14-20 in particular makes no effort to hide the challenges involved when we choose to follow Christ.

The thought of taking risks makes even the committed, mature volunteers, leaders, and staff who make up the backbone of the church a bit nervous. But since risks lie ahead for anyone who desires to follow God, we need to be ready for them.

God is a risky God, so it shouldn't surprise us that we are called to be risky too. The greatest risk was creating the earth and populating it with free-will humanoids. But he's God and he isn't scared of risk. (Actually since he knows everything, is it even risk? But maybe that's the point.)

RISKY SPIRIT

Ephesians 2:1-10 is a beautiful description of the change that took place in us when we got saved. The first verses of this passage point out that we were set free from slavery to sin and given the power to live a different kind of life.

Despite what the world portrays, there's nothing risky about living according to the urges and surges of the flesh. It's not exciting or exceptional—it's normal. It's simply the path of least resistance. If you want an original and exciting life, then buck the trends of sin and live by the Spirit.

Years ago there was a Sprite commercial that featured three tough-talking basketball players selling a fictitious sports drink. Halfway through, the commercial "stops," and an off-screen director yells out that they

RISK IS ALWAYS THE RESPONSE OF THE RIGHTEOUS.

are holding the can upside down. Instantly the hard-playing attitude disappears, and they turn out to be just stuck-up actors. One of the actors whines to the director, "'Excuse me? Excuse me? What's my motivation?"

That line stuck with me all these years, and once in awhile I'll say it to someone. They don't have any idea what I'm talking about, which makes it even funnier for me.

Actually, though, it's a good question. As Christians, why do we do what we do? Why would we even consider stepping out and taking a risk?

Here's my answer: grace is our motivation. Risk is always the response of the righteous.

Why? Because when we grasp the meaning of grace, we are released to have faith; and whenever we have faith, we naturally do good works. Look at Ephesians 2:8-10: "By grace … through faith … for good works." When you find grace in Scripture, you usually find faith there as well. Living a risky life is a natural outflow of grace.

When you understand who you are in Christ, when you realize that your righteousness before God does not depend on your achievements, you'll do what others wouldn't consider. You'll say things you wouldn't normally say. You'll go places you didn't plan to go. You'll love people others reject.

RISKY, NOT CRAZY

Don't misunderstand me—I'm not promoting some kind of crazy life. Don't be dumb in the name of being risky. Wisdom, self-control, and good judgment are part of God's nature and should be part of ours as well. True risk often means staying put and doing what you were called to, not selling everything and moving to a foreign country, unless that's what you're called to. Risk might mean eliminating something good that is taking resources away from something great. It might mean going to your son's t-ball game instead of working two more hours on a sermon.

I have a running list of indicators of a risky life. What made the list might surprise you: friendliness, happiness, encouragement, servanthood, volunteerism, generosity, sacrifice, submission, single-mindedness, and steadfastness. More than rash decisions or sensational acts, these characteristics prove to me that someone is sold out for God and living by faith.

Romans 12:1-2 says that in light of all God had done for us, risk is really not risky at all—it's rational, logical, reasonable, and appropriate. It's the natural reaction to Jesus' love and sacrifice for us.

This passage goes on to say that we need to use our gifts according to the grace given us. Practically, this is what living a risky life means—using the gifts you've been given by grace. Each of us has resources, gifts, and abilities that we still aren't employing because of fear.

A church community that understands grace and righteousness by faith will look a lot like the church in Acts 4:32-37. They healed the sick, loved the lost, gave away houses, endured persecution, preached the gospel, and grew the church.

Why did they take such a risk, and how did they find such success? The answer is simple: "great grace was upon them all." (ESV) ◼

FRIENDLINESS
HAPPINESS
ENCOURAGEMENT
SERVANTHOOD
VOLUNTEERISM
GENEROSITY
SACRIFICE
SUBMISSION
SINGLE-MINDEDNESS

+

STEADFASTNESS

THE
RIVER
OF
INTIMACY

Britt Merrick

The other night at a wedding I ran into an acquaintance, a longtime pastor of a large church. In the course of our conversation, I asked how I could pray for him. Without hesitation he said, "That I would actually spend time with Jesus and not be so caught up in being busy all the time. You'd think after all these years I'd have that down, but I don't."

Isn't it interesting how the ministry always seems to creep its way between the minister and Jesus? My friend was so busy doing things for Jesus that he didn't have much time for Jesus.

Ministry flows from intimacy. The primary call on the minister is to be with Christ in an intimate love relationship. When Jesus called the twelve disciples, He appointed them "so that they would be *with* Him and that He could send them out to preach, and to have authority to cast out the demons"[1] (emphasis mine). Note the order: Jesus ordained that His first leaders be *with* Him before they attempt to do work *for* Him. As Jesus would later teach, He is the source for life and ministry. Without deep connectivity to Him, their ability to live and lead well would crumble beneath the pressures they would soon face as leaders in His kingdom.

The same is true for the Christian leader today. We have been saved that we might have a meaningful love affair with Christ; everything else is subordinate and subsequent to that glorious truth. Tozer wrote, "We are called to an everlasting preoccupation with God."[2] Yet Christians in general, and often leaders in particular, seem to succumb to busyness and struggle with practicing unhurried intimacy with Christ.

This is a dangerous compromise. Eugene Peterson asserts, "The word *busy* is the symptom not of commitment but of betrayal. It is not devotion but defection. The adjective *busy* set as a modifier to *pastor* should sound to our ears like *adulterous* to characterize a wife or *embezzling* to characterize a banker. It is an outrageous scandal, a blasphemous affront."[3]

"Ouch," says this busy pastor.

KNOW ME TIMES THREE

In the book of Jeremiah, the Lord was expressing His displeasure with the southern kingdom of Judah: "The priests did not say, 'Where is the LORD?' And those who handle the law did not *know* Me"[4] (emphasis mine). The word *know* used here

THE WORD *BUSY* IS THE SYMPTOM NOT OF COM-MITMENT BUT OF BETRAYAL. IT IS NOT DEVOTION BUT DEFECTION … IT IS AN OUTRAGEOUS SCANDAL, A BLASPHEMOUS AFFRONT.

is the word *yada* in Hebrew, and it means to know relationally and experientially.[5]

The Lord's complaint is that they did not *know* Him relationally, experientially, and intimately. His rebuke targeted the spiritual leaders who, of all in the kingdom, carried the privilege and responsibility of knowing Him. Though many other sins were prevalent in Judah at the time, the one that seemed to most upset God was their departure from intimate relationship with Him. They were still working *for* God, but they weren't really *with* God.

We sometimes get so caught up in doing good things for God that we don't have time for God. The danger is that in our zeal and passion for the ministry, we can easily lose the *sine qua non* (essential condition) of simply knowing Christ intimately. Recall the words of the risen Lord to the church at Ephesus: "I know your deeds and your toil. … But I have this against you, that you have left your first love."[6] Their many good works were acknowledged by the Lord, but they were a pitiful substitute for relationally *loving* the Lord.

OUR LAST LOVE

Our first love is to be our last love. All that would seek to place itself between us and our first love must be dealt with ruthlessly in the life of the leader, lest he or she become weary in the numerous responsibilities facing him or her. These responsibilities, apart from connection to the Object of our service, eventually grind us down to the very core of personal inadequacy. When busyness supplants with-ness, we are in trouble.

Christ's suggested course of action for the church at Ephesus was to repent. This can mean only one thing—that the leader or minister or ministry or church that is engaged in good works while neglecting sincere relational nearness to Christ is on a perilous path and must change course immediately to avoid shipwreck. We all know that the reefs and shores of Christian work are strewn with the wrecks of busy and important, but not intimate, men and women.

The work will always seek to pry its way between Christ and the Christian. The passion of every pastor and leader must be to love and enjoy Jesus with every fiber of his or her being. Genuine and eternally impacting ministry can flow only from an intimate relationship with Christ. ◪

---

[1] Mark 3:14–15 (NASB).

[2] A. W. Tozer, *Gems from Tozer*, (Camp Hill, Penn.: Christian Publications), 13.

[3] Eugene Peterson, *The Contemplative Pastor*, (Grand Rapids, Mich.: William B. Eerdmans, 1993), 17.

[4] Jeremiah 2:8 (NASB).

[5] Warren Baker and Eugene Carpenter, *The Complete Word Study Dictionary Old Testament* (Chattanooga, Tenn.: AMG Publishers, 2003), 420.

[6] Revelation 2:2–4 (NASB).

REFLECTION

Britt eloquently draws us to the river of intimacy by nudging us out of the flow of our busyness and into the flow of right relation with Christ Jesus. The effective Christian leader must make difficult decisions regarding their time and ministry involvement. This seems to be a simple and practical fundamental of leadership, yet so many leaders struggle with stress related problems, spiritual despondency, and total burnout.

What is the culprit for this type of leadership fallout? Culture tempts the leader into chasing influence, platform, and "voice" instead of chasing silence, solitude, and a servant's heart. To overcome this pressure and to regain a fundamental spiritual foothold, we must get back to the fundamentals of our faith. Like learning to ride a bike all over again.

1
CONFESSION

Spend time in your prayer life confessing where you fall short in your relationships, in your vocation, and in your walk with Christ. Confess your selfishness. Confess your greed. Confess your lust. Lay bare your heart before Christ and He will awaken it.

2
CHALLENGE

Lean into Christ by way of study. As a leader you should not rest in your contentment to read here and there and think your spirit will be nourished. Approach your pastor and ask for one-on-one time; ask him to point you toward resources that will deepen your spiritual walk. Read broadly, not just in the leadership or ministry genres. Dig into biblical theology. Dive into a few classic novels. Spend time carving your thoughts into poems.

3
REST

Rethink how you rest. When you rest you should be renewing your mind, body, and spirit. Though sleep and relaxation revive to some extent, you can also rest by being active: take a hike by yourself—allow your body to get rid of toxins, breathe deeply, take in the solitude; go on a bike ride with your friends or family; take a few days off from digital communication gathering.

Intimacy with Christ cannot be fostered with the myriad interruptions our world throws at us. Like any other earthly relationship we must be intentional about how we cultivate our heavenly one.

WHALE
STARS

Encountering the Magnificent

TIMOTHY WILLARD AND JASON LOCY

If you ever have the chance, do yourself a favor and explore the Four Corners area where New Mexico, Colorado, Utah, and Arizona all meet. It's the kind of place that feels like God took extra care to create. In New Mexico, you can drive a hundred miles in any direction, stop the car, and step out into the resounding silence of a mesa desert where the silence hovers, permeating the entire region.

The Durango silence differs; there, Colorado's San Juan Mountains rifle up toward the sky, thick with bristle cone pines and aspens. Creeks and rivers knife down and through the mountains, splashing liquid white upon the outdoor canvas. And then there's the sound. At 4:00 a.m. on a clear June night, you can see just enough of your surroundings to feel uneasy. All is still, except for the air whistling ever so gently through the pines while the aspen leaves rustle their approval. And when you look up, through the trees, the stars jump out of the darkness like millions of surfacing whales, majestic and fearsome.

Beneath the canopy, you can barely see your campsite. If not for the whale stars, all would be black. As you stand outside your tent, you can hear your heart beating, but just barely. The silence has a rhythm — the cadence of the leaves, the flow of the rushing water, and the crackle of a neighboring fire. These are the sounds of the San Juan silence, and they are wonderfully deafening.

Next, head west, just over the mountains, to Moab, Utah. Grab some java at Mondo Coffee and hit the Porcupine Rim trail on your mountain bike or take a jeep tour of the red desert. Then, continue northwest and spend the night in Bryce Canyon.

In Bryce, another kind of silence awaits, the brilliant kind. Camp near the rim of the canyon if you can. There are plenty of sites. Do your best to wake up well before the dawn. Hike over to Sunrise Point and set up your camp chair facing east over the canyon. And wait. If you have coffee, bring it; you may also want your journal.

From this vantage point, you will be able to see more stars than you ever thought possible. They are not the same whale stars from Durango; these are the minions of God — the infinite army of light soldiers, their shields shimmering like a pirate's treasure. They're a spectacle so vivid you can decipher them by color and size. But this is not why you're sitting here.

As the sun gets closer to the horizon, the stars fade and the canyon begins to wake. All the hoodoo rock formations with their red-rock hues come into view, and you begin to see the valley stretch out before you. The thin mountain air crystallizes the view. And then it happens: the first peek of sunlight emerges, shouting past the horizon like a growling giant. The canyon explodes with color. The sky bleeds into a rainbow while the canyon dances in shadows and light.

The sound is brilliant, painted with color and majesty and wonder, and a touch of magic. As you watch it all unfold, you gasp. Again, you can hear your heart beating, fast. You breathe in while your eyes dart from canyon to sun to sky to journal. Nothing more to do but sit and listen and watch.

The weight of silence, the fullness of solitude — we are not familiar with either. They seem strange and un-

comfortable to us. And yet within them are the deep murmurings of God.

You will, undoubtedly, be hard pressed to find a place devoid of sound, so perhaps the better idea of silence rests in the act of being quiet, hushing your words to hear God's. And doing so in a place of beauty, removed from distractions.

The Four Corners' version of silence and solitude is grand. Its massiveness makes you feel insignificant. If you've ever rappelled down a sheer Sierra Nevada cliff or dropped two hundred feet into the pitch black belly of a mountain, then you know the feeling of complete helplessness — your heart beating in your ears, your mind racing through death scenarios. Fear and exhilaration fill the encounter. The allure of this part of the country rests in its wildness and unpredictability. At any moment, you could be crushed by its immensity. It drips with holy grandeur, like God is hovering over and breathing down on the land.

PATH TO SELF-ABANDONMENT
Who is God to you?

When you daily approach him, how do you do it? What motivates you? Do you come to him with a scripted mindset as if you were taking a vacation to Disney World where you know exactly what to expect? Do you bank on God being and acting a certain way?

Or do you approach him with zero expectations? The same way you'd approach hiking a newfound trail. You would start walking, taking in the view. Nothing scripted, nothing predictable.

What do you bring before him? Do you bring him the cracked vessel of *you*? Or do you bring him a veneered you, the lost and afraid you?

What does it mean to worship him?

Too often we treat God as our pocket Savior, our own personal Jesus, our political fail-safe, or maybe even our get-out-of-jail-free card for a way of living we know isn't on the up and up.

BEHOLD, THE DWELLING PLACE OF GOD IS WITH MAN. — **REVELATION 21:3 ESV**

"If you have only come the length of asking God for things," writes minister and teacher Oswald Chambers, "you have never come to the first strand of abandonment, you have become a Christian from a standpoint of your own."[1] And this will not fly. We cannot approach God as though he were a cosmic superstore. We must be willing to hold the relational position of self-abandonment.

Self-abandonment? Isn't this the society in which the pursuit of self gets rewarded? Do we not promote language like "positive self-speak" and "leveraging influence" and "expressing yourself"? In our society, if you're not leveraging or maximizing something, you're underachieving.

But no matter how much we try to skew the Christian life, we cannot wiggle away from Christ's own challenge to his disciples: "If anyone would come after me, let him deny himself and take up his cross and follow me."[2] Through Christ we find that grace transforms us out of our fallenness and that mercy challenges us to follow after Christ himself, a way of life wholly other.

Life's realities make following along this narrow path difficult. It can be lonely. We'd rather be friends with God and fall into a nonchalant faith of church attendance and worship events than to seek him in the brilliant silence. Many of us are frustrated in our spiritual lives because we feel like God doesn't hear us. But should that frustration surprise us when we ask of him from a position of selfishness?

Seventy-five years ago, poet T. S. Eliot wrote,
O world of spring and autumn, birth and dying!
The endless cycle of idea and action,
Endless invention, endless experiment,
Brings knowledge of motion, but not of stillness;
Knowledge of speech, but not of silence;
Knowledge of words, and ignorance of the Word.
All our knowledge brings us nearer to death,
But nearness to death no nearer to God.
Where is the Life we have lost in living?
Where is the wisdom we have lost in knowledge?
Where is the knowledge we have lost in information?

The cycles of Heaven in twenty centuries
Brings us farther from God and nearer to the Dust.[3]

Eliot's words are familiar to us. Not because we have read them before but because we have lived them and *are* living them. In gaining the world, we refuse to abandon the self. We are nearer to the dust and have nothing to show for it.

A TRUE ENCOUNTER

To encounter the grandeur of the Four Corners, you have to go there. And when you do, the heavy silence and vast solitude are waiting, by-products of the journey to this splendid destination. God should be a daily destination for us. He should be one with whom we seek audience, a place we long to be in, a river we seek to wash in, a canyon we want to get lost in.

We need to go *to* God and then stop. We need to lay down our burdens and requests for a moment and attempt to gather him in, encountering his vastness. We do not approach him with a laundry list of wants. Rather, we approach him in order to worship him — giving him his worth — hoping that by being in his presence, we will glean a small piece of his glory to season our daily existence.

But our society makes it difficult for us to fully understand what it means to encounter God in this way. We use personal *experience* as our doping needle for the transcendent. We think that if we can manipulate experiences, the world will feel better. We will *be* better.

We pile our experiences high, and though they shape us to some extent, they do not understand or know us. Experiences are great but by definition they are merely emotional, self-focused events.[4] They leave us just as alone as we were before. If we focus only on experience, we miss the most important part of the life equation: *encounter.*

Think about the whale stars. Think about peeking through the ponderosa pine and seeing a few falling stars light up the sky. After it happens, you feel like you have to tell someone; you feel like you just stole something so beautiful from the sky and you can't even explain why. You're dizzy with excitement.

That's how our interaction with God should be. When we seek *encounters* with God, we never know what to expect. He's as unpredictable as a fall day in the Colorado Rockies. Why can't our worship gatherings reflect this truth about God? Maybe because most of us like to plan for God like we plan for the weather.

When we make worship a sensory experience, we devalue its authenticity. The primary focus, which should be on God, turns to those manipulating the experience. God doesn't speak to us through the cool of culture; he speaks in gentle whispers. What would happen to the church if we walked in on Sunday open and broken before God, ready to encounter his ravishing Spirit and Word?

Unlike *experience*, the word *encounter* carries a relational meaning. It can mean "a chance meeting" or "a hostile confrontation." Is God more an event that we attend in order to accumulate knowledge or is he a being whom we meet with or even clash with? Does he reveal himself throughout the world in creation and through his Word? Do we not have very deep ways to come up against his vast and untamed glory?

When we attend worship services that allow us to stop in and see God, who is he *really* to us? Is he not more than this?

Who is God if not the divine Father whom we encounter with awe and reverence, fire devouring before him and around him a tempest raging?[5] Who is God if not the Son, the head of the church, whom we encounter together, corporately, speaking truth and love to one another, growing into him who is our Head?[6]

Who is God if not the Holy Spirit, whom we encounter within—our Great Teacher, Counselor, and Reminder of Truth.[7] God did not create humankind to *experience* us and then walk away. He created humankind to walk with us, to love us, and for us to be loved by him.

BARKING LINES

When we talk about encounter, we must address the relational element. Think about life as if it were one giant conversation. Conversation is a dialogue between two or more people, which makes those we live with and among a part of the dialogue. There is give and take, reciprocity, and confrontation. We serve the conversation when we listen, considering the other person's needs more important than our own. It can be a beautiful dance.

But when we live experientially, the dialogue breaks down; it becomes one-sided, a monologue. In a monologue, only one person speaks, only one person matters. A monologuer does not stand in a position of true relationship. He stands alone, barking lines to everyone.

It's the same in life. If we live like the monologuer, we begin to use people as leverage devices, seen only for their use to our particular needs. Our interactions with them turn into a power, dominance, and manipulation structure and less of a relationship. The monologuer does not need interaction, because he just wants to control people and events. To the monologuer, people exist as a means to success. He does not understand others, nor is he understood. He speaks, and lives, to hear his own voice.[8]

Is this how we interact with God? We fail to realize that he originated the dialogue and that he longs to interact with us. The fact that we can have real interaction with the God of the universe is staggering. It's a reality that comes to life when you walk outside during a fall sunset, see the colors, and whisper to God. Eyes filling up and heart bursting, you hear his voice. You shudder.

The monologuer sees the world as his audience, a stage meant only for him. He speaks from a position "of his own." Stiff and rigid, brash and bold, the monologuer misses the beauty and romance of dialogue with God. For there must be tender compliance as we speak to and with God. As the Teacher reminds us in Ecclesiastes, we must come first to listen, keeping our words few and our hearts open, ready for the radiance of the Father.[9]

* * *

The Four Corners area feels like a frontier we can all learn from — just wild enough to scare us a bit but tame enough to invite us in. The greatest part about it is you cannot turn to leave when you start to feel uncomfortable. If you abide there long enough, you will find all your secret thoughts exposed, waving in the mountain air. No place for veneer; no place for selfish desires. Just you and God, if you dare encounter him, if you dare enter into conversation with him. ◼

[1] Oswald Chambers, *My Utmost for His Highest* (Uhrichsville: Barbour Books, 1963), 118.

[2] Matt. 16:24 ESV

[3] T. S. Eliot, "Choruses from the Rock," 1934.

[4] *Experience* as defined in *The American Heritage Dictionary*: "*n.* The apprehension of an object, thought, or emotion through the sense or mind. Active participation in events or activities, lead to the accumulation of knowledge. *v.* To participate in personally." Even by definition, we find the idea of experiencing God to be self-focused.

[5] Ps. 50:3 NIV

[6] Eph. 4:6 NIV

[7] John 14:26 NIV

[8] Alistair McFadyen, *The Call to Personhood* (Cambridge: Cambridge Univ. Press, 1990), 113–26.

[9] Eccl. 5:2.

REFLECTION

Take a few moments and read aloud Psalm 104. You might also want to read the creation account in Genesis 1-2 since this Psalm is a reflective commentary on those events. As you're reading the Psalm, take time to reflect on God's creation: the cosmos, the earth, you.

What thoughts did you have during that reading?

How does this description of God align with your view of him?

Compare God's grandness to modern celebrity. How does it compare?

DISCUSSION

Does your church focus more on communicating relevance through the language of culture, such as putting major emphasis on creating a cool environment, snappy programming, and topical preaching? Or does it focus on the worship of God through reverent worship, joyful fellowship, and exegetical preaching?

Do you agree or disagree with the authors' view regarding encounter versus experience? Why or why not? Can you support your view?

What does Oswald Chambers mean when he uses the term *self-abandonment*? Which side of self-abandonment are you on? What in our society makes it hard to sacrifice your own personal desires?

If everyone could look at your personal and family priorities, what would they discover about you that they don't already know? Would you be proud or embarrassed about this?

APPLICATION

In the gospels we find Jesus escaping the crowds and even his friends in order to spend time in prayer and communion with his heavenly Father. You may think you're not wired that way, or perhaps you love to escape. Either way, this month make it a priority to get out in God's creation for some reflection. If you have a family, be sensitive and set up a play day for your kids at a friend's house. Or escape in the early morning. It does not have to be extreme, like a week-long spiritual retreat. Take baby steps. Go to a nearby park in the morning. Head down to the local lake or river. Or just take a late evening walk under the stars.

During your mini-retreats focus on prayer—two-way prayer where you spend time just listening for God's voice in your heart. Spend time confessing things you know are hanging around in your heart. If you want, take a devotional along for some guided reading and reflection. But the main point of getting away is just to *be* and to see and to hear the voice of God in your surroundings.

PSALM 8

LORD, our Lord,
how majestic is your name in all the earth!

You have set your glory
in the heavens.
Through the praise of children and infants
you have established a stronghold against your enemies,
to silence the foe and the avenger.
When I consider your heavens,
the work of your fingers,
the moon and the stars,
which you have set in place,
what is mankind that you are mindful of them,
human beings that you care for them?

You have made them a little lower than the angels
and crowned them with glory and honor.
You made them rulers over the works of your hands;
you put everything under their feet:
all flocks and herds,
and the animals of the wild,
the birds in the sky,
and the fish in the sea,
all that swim the paths of the seas.

LORD, our Lord,
how majestic is your name in all the earth!
(NIV)

THE UN GLAMOROUS

WALK OF THE HUMBLE

Esther Fleece

In your twenties and thirties, life can sometimes feel like an endless ride. At the same time, there's pressure to find your niche in the world, or at least I've felt the squeeze. For Christians, this often translates to "calling"—the call to marriage and family, to a place to live, to a community of friends, and to work. In a very real sense, this pressure honors God, especially if we're actively working out a biblical calling, and we're ever-aware that life is "not about us."

Most of us get stuck at one time or another. We become preoccupied with receiving a "lightning-bolt moment," and the quest to walk into the thing that will make our hearts leap with anticipation, purpose, and joy. Surely God will send us a direct message, here and now!

And while we're waiting for some divine sign about our calling, we spend our time toiling away at what we feel is some random job. And we hang out on Facebook, watch endless episodes of *Glee* or *The Bachelor,* swing with our core friends at Starbucks, and wring our hands from time to time over the perceived silence of God. Look, I've been there, people.

SEEING THE NEED

In high school it was about college for me, and choosing just the right major. And after college it was about biding my time until the Lord opened the door to meaningful ministry. I was faithful in a job that I believed was taking me nowhere instead of seeing it as a place to sow into the lives of my coworkers, and as preparation for the future.

I wasted a lot of time, and missed out on enjoying or being fully present in the season God had me in.

Let's face the facts: We live in a world of need. We all know that, right? And I'm not just talking about issues like global poverty, sex-trafficking, and orphans in developing countries. Right outside our front door there are desperate, lonely, hurting people—human beings lacking hope—and as a basic tenet of our faith we are called to do something about it.

If you pray for the Lord to make you aware of the need, He'll bring people out of the woodwork. I guarantee it.

The hardship may manifest in the barista or sales staff person you work with. Did you know that he or she

"HUMILITY IS NOT THINKING LESS OF YOURSELF, IT'S THINKING OF YOURSELF LESS. HUMILITY IS THINKING MORE OF OTHERS. HUMBLE PEOPLE ARE SO FOCUSED ON SERVING OTHERS, THEY DON'T THINK OF THEMSELVES."

–RICK WARREN

struggles with crippling depression? Or it may manifest with the weary looking parents at church with the adopted kids, or the elderly woman in the apartment upstairs who just doesn't get out much. It could also be volunteering at a small struggling ministry downtown, a great place to be fully utilized and cut your teeth on a variety of projects.

I've found that calling is usually not big or flashy; for most it's unglamorous, obscure, and persistently difficult. But through the rough seas, the Lord undoubtedly molds our character and makes us more like Himself. What a crazy important truth.

GET ACTIVE

One of my favorite verses in the Bible is Micah 6:8. I believe this is a perfect lens in which to see this topic. *"He has shown you, O mortal, what is good. And what does the Lord require of you? To act justly and to love mercy and to walk humbly with your God."* (NIV)

I love that this verse is so active. The Lord requires us to act, to love, and to walk humbly with Him. If we're not doing this—if we're not aware of what's happening around us, and the opportunities He puts in our path every day—we're not living faithfully.

But a prelude to any action is gaining perspective (and praying up). First and foremost it's the head and heart knowledge that life is *not* about you. It's *not* about your satisfaction, your comfort, your personal fulfillment, or your success. For the Christian it's all about Jesus. It's about faithfulness in the details of life; trusting Him in every season; and living in authentic humility.

As Pastor Rick Warren says, "Humility is not thinking less of yourself, it's thinking of yourself less. Humility is thinking more of others. Humble people are so focused on serving others, they don't think of themselves." I love that. It's leaving the house each morning with that perspective, even though the application is truly a lifelong battle.

Speaking of which, not having it be all about you and me can be a tough nut to crack. After all, we've been raised in a society where it *is* about us, our needs and our happiness. From the time we are wee babies, it's ingrained in our DNA. It's revered by our culture. Unfortunately, as Christians, we've not faced this sin directly; rather we've wrapped it up in noble, even heroic language about Christian service. And oftentimes our motives are mixed: We serve out of love for Jesus *and* a drive to gratify ourselves. We have to examine our hearts day-by-day, season-by-season.

WHAT HE DESIRES

So what's the bottom line? The Lord longs to satisfy our desires as long as they are aligned with His. He wants to use our specific gifts—gifts that we may not even know about yet. And He wants our hearts to sing over the prospect of serving Him, however challenging.

The coolest part of the process is that the Lord honors our dependability in the small things and in all seasons. Remember, "He who calls you is faithful; He will surely do it" (1 Thessalonians 5:24 ESV). He leads us, He calls us, and He is faithful to complete this process we are in.

In this season, and hopefully the next, I want to be a person who strives to be more concerned in living out daily faithfulness and obedience to my King, rather than writing my five-year plan or contemplating my next move. God is not working all things out for my happiness, but for His purposes. **◧**

REFLECTION

Many of my friends have struggled with plans over the future; especially in this economy, it can be a stressful subject. Sometimes they glaze over when the discussion of God's calling comes up, or they admit to just being plain confused with the process or what Jesus may be saying to them.

You may be faced with several decisions right now, all of which may be great possibilities. "But which one is my *true* calling?" you ask. "How do I make this decision? It's killing me." For all you pragmatists out there, here are three things that you can begin to think through and answer on a personal level. If you're doing a group study, break up into groups of three and walk through these concepts together.

1
DISCONNECT + RECENTER

Take a few moments and read Mark Batterson's interview. Mark says that unless we are willing to institute parameters on our schedule and our use of social media technologies, we will not be fit for ministry. If you need to make an important decision regarding your vocational calling or just need to return to a deeper walk with Christ, then you need to make some changes; maybe some radical ones.

Take inventory of your time. How much time do you spend trolling the Internet or checking email or updating your various feeds? If this time allotment is inordinate, then you need to make a major change and re-establish your calendar priorities. In the meantime, however, you simply need to take a break from the digital world for a few days.

Are you honoring the Sabbath day of rest as Jesus commanded? Are you carving out time, multiple times a day, to commune with God, to hear His voice, and to meditate on His Word?

2
FAST + PRAY

Fasting has taken a nosedive in our latte-loving culture. Some think that a fast consists of taking a week off of their latte intake; or perhaps taking a break from football (God forbid). If we look at Scripture we find that fasting was common among the Jews and the early Christians. Christ Himself fasted and prayed in order to have intimate communion with His Father.

Pick up Richard Foster's *Celebration of the Disciplines* and read the chapter on fasting. Foster gives scriptural support for fasting and delineates on how fasting and prayer are related. He also tells a couple of stories of how fasting helped to clarify his mind and spirit with regard to a decision he needed to make.

How often do you fast? Do you know how to fast? If you've fasted before, what did you learn?

3
LISTEN + DO

My namesake, Queen Esther, is a role model when it comes to hearing the Lord and acting upon it. In the midst of preparing to be Queen of Persia, she was urged by her adoptive father Mordecai to step out and save the lives of the her people. I'm certain that risking life and limb didn't top her "to-do" list or fit into her vision of the future.

How did she react? The Bible says she was terrified, but it didn't stop her from taking the next step. She prayed and fasted for three days, and enlisted others to do the same. Then hearing from God, Esther stepped forward and acted on His calling.

So, if you follow these three steps will you see the future clearly or will it make your decisions any easier? Maybe. Remember that our faith is shrouded in mystery and our trust in the Lord in the midst of the process is honoring to Him. Most of all, though, God is concerned about our relationship with Him, rather than what we may or may not do for the Kingdom. And engaging in spiritual practices such as fasting, prayer, and walking by faith leads to a deeper friendship with God. In the end, that beats a dream job any day!

TORN

YET TRUSTING

Jud Wilhite

A thirty-year-old woman approached me after a weekend service. She looked like she was carrying the weight of the world on her shoulders. She said, "Jud, I have a friend at work who is going blind. All of my associates are saying she's going blind because of sin in her life. They say she's going blind because her parents sinned and made mistakes or because she's sinned and made mistakes. Can that be true?"

I was privileged to open the Bible to the scene where Jesus was walking with his disciples and they asked him that very question after encountering a man born blind:

> "Rabbi," his disciples asked him, "why was this man born blind? Was it because of his own sins or his parents' sins?" "It was not because of his sins or his parents' sins," Jesus answered. "This happened so the power of God could be seen in him."[1]

After I read this passage to her, I looked up at her face to see tears rolling down her cheeks. She smiled and gave me the biggest bear hug.

It took me a while to realize exactly what was going on, but at last it dawned on me. I said, "It's not your friend who's going blind, is it?"

"No," she said. "I've lost eighty percent of my vision, and the next twenty will go soon."

I said, "Let me tell you what the Bible says. This has nothing to do with specific sin in the life of your parents or in your own life. I don't know why you are facing this, but I believe you can trust God in it. God can use what you are going through to bring glory to him even in the midst of your struggle."

As she wiped the tears from her face, she was smiling ear to ear. Later, when I saw her around the church, she looked like a different person. She reminds me of Jesus' words "The truth will set you free."[2]

Wrong assumptions about God and suffering had caused her serious pain. When we make the false and formulaic assumption that pain and suffering are always a punishment for a specific sin, we end up making the ways of God sound more like karma. Yes, there is such a thing as reaping what you sow, and there is such a thing as suffering the consequences of our actions. But the idea that all sickness or sad circumstances are the result of a specific sin positions God not as a loving Father who oversees our suffering and comforts us in it,

WE ALL SUFFER IN THIS MESSED-UP WORLD. BUT THIS DOESN'T MEAN GOD'S GRACE IS BEYOND US OR UNAVAILABLE TO US.

but as an abusive Father who administers our suffering and stands over us with a hair-trigger temper. And the Bible flat-out says we are not destined for wrath.[3]

Yet unfortunately these kinds of assumptions are all too real around the water coolers of our world. These falsehoods stir up doubt and pain in the minds of those who suffer. But they stem from and feed into our worst fears and misguided assumptions when we are suffering: Is my condition due to my specific sin? Did my parents do something wrong that I'm gonna pay for the rest of my life? Does my pain prove I'll never be forgiven by God?

GUILT TRIPPING

When we are torn, we must choose to live by faith in the revealed Word of God over the assumptions of people. It may be that we have brought our difficulty on ourselves by our actions. God may be disciplining us as his children in these moments because he loves us. But he's not getting even for a particular sin.

Many of us assume we understand God's forgiveness and grace, but when trouble comes, we often walk around feeling condemned. We assume that God's grace doesn't reach to us.

For years I lived in the odd limbo of believing in God and his grace while still feeling like I was not forgiven. No matter what I did, I couldn't seem to shake the sense that my past addictions and mistakes condemned me. It drove me to the performance treadmill, where I tried harder and harder to earn the love of God. When I wasn't on that treadmill, I was often wallowing in pointless guilt, because no matter how much I tried, I kept failing. And my past was always there.

One thing I needed was to see that my own refusal to accept grace was actually self-pity and pride. I had always viewed it as somehow righteous, like I didn't deserve grace fully because of my past. But when I realized that my refusal to accept God's forgiveness was actually the height of arrogance and pride and could stir the anger of God, well, that was something else. It rattled me.

In refusing to accept grace, I'm saying my word is better than God's Word. I'm saying the cross of Jesus was not enough for me. I'm saying his death and sacrifice should have been greater. God has to do more for my sins to be forgiven. I was trapped in unhealthy guilt.

UNHEALTHY GUILT

There is a difference between healthy and unhealthy guilt. Healthy guilt motivates us to mend relationships, make things right, and move toward health. It is focused on others more than on oneself. Unhealthy guilt often results in self-hatred. We condemn ourselves. We refuse to believe we can ever be accepted.

Unhealthy guilt and shame are debilitating. I once encountered a man who was so broken from self-hatred that he was coming unglued. He said that he had prayed every day for God to forgive him for something he had done ten years earlier.

I told him to read Psalm 51, which is David's prayer for forgiveness after committing the sins of adultery, murder, lying, and covering it all up. I challenged him to read it and ask for forgiveness. Then I said, "After asking forgiveness, don't ever ask God to forgive you for that sin again."

He was shocked and took a step back.

PSALM 51

Read all of this Psalm. What guilt are you dealing with that is keeping you from being present in the every day? How does guilt affect our relationships with our family? Friends? Coworkers? As you read, make this Psalm your prayer to be free from your sin guilt.

Generous in love—God, give grace!
  Huge in mercy—wipe out my bad record.
Scrub away my guilt,
  soak out my sins in your laundry.
I know how bad I've been;
  my sins are staring me down.

You're the One I've violated, and you've seen
  it all, seen the full extent of my evil.
You have all the facts before you;
  whatever you decide about me is fair.
I've been out of step with you for a long time,
  in the wrong since before I was born.
What you're after is truth from the inside out.
  Enter me, then; conceive a new, true life.

Soak me in your laundry and I'll come out clean,
  scrub me and I'll have a snow-white life.
Tune me in to foot-tapping songs,
  set these once-broken bones to dancing.
Don't look too close for blemishes,
  give me a clean bill of health.
God, make a fresh start in me,
  shape a Genesis week from the chaos of my life.

Don't throw me out with the trash,
  or fail to breathe holiness in me.
Bring me back from gray exile,
  put a fresh wind in my sails!
Give me a job teaching rebels your ways
  so the lost can find their way home.
Commute my death sentence, God, my salvation God,
  and I'll sing anthems to your life-giving ways.
Unbutton my lips, dear God;
  I'll let loose with your praise.

Going through the motions doesn't please you,
  a flawless performance is nothing to you.
I learned God-worship
  when my pride was shattered.
Heart-shattered lives ready for love
  don't for a moment escape God's notice.

Make Zion the place you delight in,
  repair Jerusalem's broken-down walls.
Then you'll get real worship from us,
  acts of worship small and large,
Including all the bulls
  they can heave onto your altar!
(MSG)

"HE HAS REMOVED OUR SINS AS FAR FROM US AS THE EAST IS FROM THE WEST." THE COOL THING IS YOU CAN GO TO ABSOLUTE NORTH AND SOUTH, BUT THERE IS NO ABSOLUTE EAST OR WEST. HE HAS REMOVED OUR SINS FROM US AS FAR AS IS POSSIBLE. IT'S TRUE THAT WE ARE COMMANDED TO CONFESS OUR SINS, AND WE SHOULD DO THAT, BUT LET'S STOP BRINGING UP THE SINS OF OLD THAT GOD HAS ALREADY FORGIVEN US FOR.

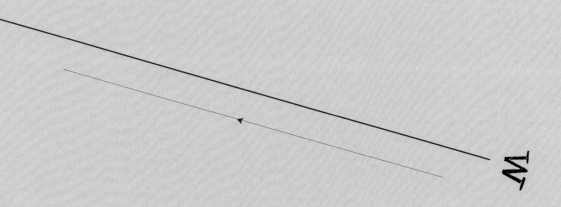

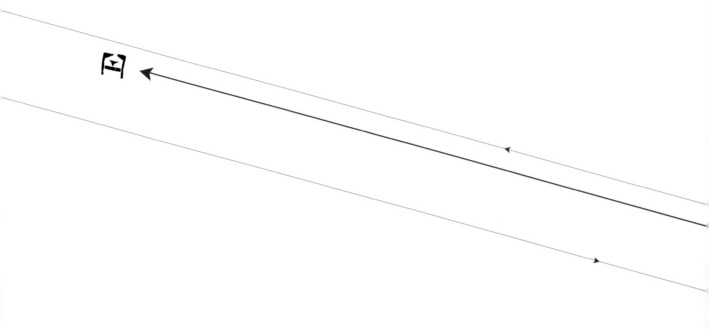

So I said it again, "As your pastor, I'm telling you, ask forgiveness once more and don't ever ask God to forgive you for that sin again. He's already forgiven you. He's let it go, but you keep bringing it up every morning."

I shared with him that the Bible says, "He has removed our sins as far from us as the east is from the west."[4] The cool thing is you can go to absolute north and south, but there is no absolute east or west. He has removed our sins from us as far as is possible. It's true that we are commanded to confess our sins, and we should do that, but let's stop bringing up the sins of old that God has already forgiven us for.

When we're torn, we'll be tempted to doubt God's grace in many ways. So we should take heart that salvation is a gift of faith. We can't earn it and we won't lose it due to our troubles.

We all suffer in this messed-up world. But this doesn't mean God's grace is beyond us or unavailable to us. What if we reevaluated our assumptions with the Bible? What if we clung to his word that there is "no condemnation for those who belong to Christ Jesus"?[5] What if we made the choice right now to let our assumptions be guided by God's Word and let our trial guide us to greater love and dependence on God? ⊂

[1] John 9:2-3 NLT.

[2] John 8:32 NLT.

[3] 1 Thessalonians 5:9 NLT.

[4] Psalm 103:12 NLT.

[5] Romans 8:1 NLT.

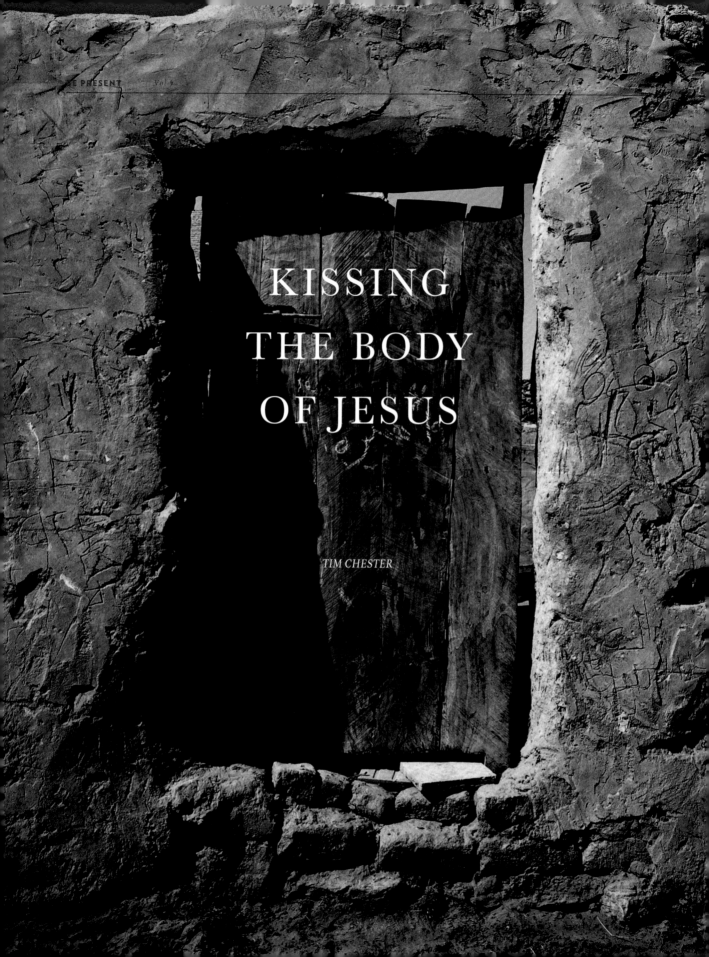

KISSING

THE BODY

OF JESUS

TIM CHESTER

In Luke we read the following story about a dinner party.

> *One of the Pharisees asked him to eat with him, and he went into the Pharisee's house and took his place at the table. And behold, a woman of the city, who was a sinner, when she learned that he was reclining at table in the Pharisee's house, brought an alabaster flask of ointment, and standing behind him at his feet, weeping, she began to wet his feet with her tears and wiped them with the hair of her head and kissed his feet and anointed them with the ointment. Now when the Pharisee who had invited him saw this, he said to himself, "If this man were a prophet, he would have known who and what sort of woman this is who is touching him, for she is a sinner."*
> (Luke 7:36–39 ESV)

Luke's presentation of this meal seems to reflect the Greco-Roman *symposium*—a meal followed by an extended discussion. The diners reclined around three sides of a central table on couches, leaving the fourth side open to allow servants access to the table. Bread and wine would be on the table, along with a main dish into which you dipped your bread. Diners lay in a semi-recumbent position with their legs out behind them.

Homes in the time of Jesus—especially large homes—had semi-public areas. Some rooms opened onto a courtyard that outsiders could enter. Visitors could see what was happening and even contribute to what was being said. People could readily come in off the streets to pay their respects to the householder or to transact business. The poor, too, might hang around hoping for leftovers.

With this in mind it's easier to picture how this story unfolded. The woman is probably loitering in the public area, and then slips into the dining room and starts rubbing Jesus' feet as they stretch out behind him on the couch.

But this is the home of a Pharisee, and the Pharisees guarded their purity closely. The Promised Land was defiled by Roman occupation, but at least they could keep their own bodies pure, ready for the day of liberation. So they avoided contact with those they considered impure—like this sinful woman. To the Pharisees she is like an infectious disease. Yet Jesus accepts her. He demonstrates God's grace by welcoming sinners.

And that's okay by us. Christians love a good before-and-after story. You know the sort of thing: "Before I met Christ I was a drug addict and criminal, but now my life has changed."

But this woman treats Jesus with a shocking degree of intimacy. This is not appropriate public behavior. She lets down her hair to wipe her tears from Jesus' feet. In that culture, letting down your hair was what you did in the bedroom. "Letting her hair down in this setting would have been on a par with appearing topless in public."[2]

Then the woman kisses Jesus' feet and pours perfume on them. There's even a suggestion that she's treating Jesus as a client, possibly the only way she knows how to relate to men. But Jesus doesn't stop her.

Prostitution, if that was her business, is a commercial parody of hospitality. But Jesus recognizes her actions as the real thing. He reinterprets what she does as a loving act rather than an erotic act.

Jesus doesn't stop her, even though his reputation is at stake (Luke 7:39). Jesus is happy to link his identity to hers—just as he is happy to link his identity to yours and mine.

Luke seems to pick stories involving tax collectors and prostitutes. They exemplify notorious sinners. It's as if he's testing us. Have we grasped God's grace? How do we react when a promiscuous woman kisses the body of Jesus? Do we celebrate God's grace, or are we scandalized? The grace of God turns out to be uncomfortable and embarrassing. Jesus is socially disruptive; his radical grace disrupts social situations. And we don't like church to be disrupted. We regard marginalized people in the church as "a problem" to be "handled."

Involvement with people, especially the marginalized, begins with a profound grasp of God's grace. Often our instincts are to keep our distance. But the Son of God ate with them. He's not embarrassed by them. He lets them kiss his feet.

SINNERS WELCOME JESUS
There are two sides to this story in Luke 7. It's not only a story of Jesus welcoming sinners; it's also a story of a sinner welcoming Jesus. Tim Costello tells how he was

looking at this story with a group of drug addicts and prostitutes in Melbourne, Australia.

One of the prostitutes said, "Jesus must've been a really great bloke." She could imagine what it was like for this woman. She thought of the formal evenings at the big houses in the posh suburbs of Melbourne. She thought about party-crashing one of those parties, of how she would be treated. She could understand what it cost this woman to anoint the feet of Jesus. She could imagine the repulsion directed toward her by other guests. She could hear the mutterings and see the glares. She could feel the threat of violence. She could understand how much this woman must have loved Jesus.

Twice Luke tells us that this party took place in the home of a Pharisee (Luke 7:36–37). Luke emphasizes the location. This is Simon's house. And that means Simon is the host. Or is he?

Today a host might shake guests' hands, take their coats, and offer them something to drink. In Jesus' time, you offered water for their feet and greeted them with a kiss. But Simon does none of these things. He is *the host who's not really a host.* Instead the woman is *the host who's not even a guest.* She's a party-crasher. Jesus contrasts Simon's hospitality with hers:

> » *You* gave me no water for my feet, but *she* has wet my feet with her tears and wiped them with her hair.
> » *You* gave me no kiss, but from the time I came in *she* has not ceased to kiss my feet.
> » *You* did not anoint my head with oil, but *she* has anointed my feet with ointment.

She's the one who welcomed Jesus—not Simon. And it's not even her house. Jesus says: "Do you see this woman?" (v. 44). I think we can safely assume Simon had noticed her! But Jesus is contrasting this woman with "your house." "I am in *your* house, but *she's* been my host."

DEPTH OF FORGIVENESS
So why does she do it? Perhaps she sees in Simon's treatment of Jesus something of the way in which she has been treated. Simon is only interested in Jesus for his entertainment value—the eccentric preacher and miracle worker was the

must-have guest on the social circuit. He doesn't care for Jesus as a person. This woman could relate to that. She was used to being used by men without respect.

But there's something more going on. Jesus says her faith has saved her (Luke 7:50). What she does is a response of faith to something she's heard or seen in Jesus. Maybe he's cured her from some sickness. Or maybe she's heard him telling people not to condemn others, but to forgive (6:37).

What's the difference, then, between these two people? To the onlookers the answer is obvious. One is a righteous, respectable man; the other is a degraded, sinful woman who sells herself for money. But Jesus sees things altogether differently. When Simon condemns Jesus, Jesus responds not by defending his actions, but by explaining hers.

> *And Jesus answering said to him, "Simon, I have something to say to you." And he answered, "Say it, Teacher." "A certain moneylender had two debtors. One owed five hundred denarii, and the other fifty. When they could not pay, he cancelled the debt of both. Now which of them will love him more?" Simon answered, "The one, I suppose, for whom he cancelled the larger debt." And he said to him, "You have judged rightly."* (Luke 7:40-43 ESV)

The principle is simple. If someone forgives you, you'll love them. If someone forgives you a lot, you'll love them a lot. Even Simon concedes this. And this woman clearly loves Jesus a lot. Her audacity, her tears, and her affection for Jesus make that clear. So Jesus can say with confidence that her sins are forgiven.

But what about Simon? Simon hasn't even shown the normal courtesies of a host to Jesus, and he's despised this poor woman. He hasn't shown love. The only conclusion can be that he's been forgiven little—and probably not

at all. Simon is not only a legalist, but has structured his world around his legalism. Meals express inclusion. But this meal has been warped by legalism. Simon wants his meals to express the wrong kind of inclusion. Simon thinks he's invited the righteous, so the unrighteous are forced to party-crash. But Jesus reveals that Simon's definition of righteousness is upside down.

Simon's attitude to this woman exposes his heart. Problem people, difficult people, different people have a habit of exposing our hearts. Behavior always comes from the desires of the heart—Jesus says as much in the previous chapter (Luke 6:43–45). When a fellow ministry leader and I faced a difficult situation, he said, "What I find most disappointing is what it has revealed about my own heart. It's shown me again that I still need people's approval, because I fear them more than I fear God." When someone is difficult, disappointing, or disrespectful, your reaction reveals your own heart. If you react with anger or bitterness, then your "need" for control or respect or success is exposed.

If you're trusting God's sovereignty rather than your own abilities, and if you're concerned for God's glory rather than your own reputation, then it will be a different story. When you discover that someone in your church has fallen into sin, your own heart will be exposed. You may discover grace in your heart from God. But you may also discover pride and self-righteousness.

Whenever we look down on someone for being smelly, or disorganized, or lazy, or emotional, or promiscuous, or socially inept, or bitter, then we're like graceless Simon. And if we look down on people for not understanding grace, then we are like graceless Simon. If you're thinking about how this applies to someone else, then you're like Simon. Jesus says to us, "If you look down on others, you love little, because you understand so little of your sin and my grace." ∎

1. Joel E. Green, The Gospel of Luke, New International Commentary on the New Testament (Grand Rapids, MI: Eerdmans, 1997), 305, 309.
2. Ibid., 310.
3. Ibid., 309.
4. John Nolland, Luke 1: 9-20, vol. 35A, Word Biblical Commentary (Nashville: Thomas Nelson, 1989), 355.

Taken from *A Meal With Jesus* by Tim Chester (c) 2011. Used by permission of Crossway, a publishing ministry of Good News Publishers, Wheaton, Il 60187, www.crossway.org

REFLECTION

If we want to participate in true community we must be willing to be authentic with others. Understanding that authenticity is a current buzz word within the church culture, let's set that aside for a moment and think about what true community looks like. A true community involves sharing our lives with one another—a willingness to move beyond the surface of cliches and facts and enter into the realm of our personal hopes, dreams, fears, and struggles. True community involves sharing our lives at a level of vulnerability and intimacy which is very rare in our world today, yet if we are honest, is something that we all deeply desire.

It's difficult enough to enter into this level of relationship with others we have an affinity for, but what about those that are nothing like us? What about those with whom we have nothing in common? Even more so, what about those that society has marginalized or rejected? Do we welcome them into our immediate community? As we are shown in this story from Luke, Jesus sure did. One of the definitions of community provided by dictionary.com is very telling in saying that a community is, "a group ... perceived or perceiving itself as distinct in some respect from the larger society within which it exists." By showing the love and grace of Christ to the marginalized we provide tangible evidence to our society that there is a community that exists whose values are upside down from the values of this world. We become a community of grace which provides a powerful signpost for the Kingdom that is to come.

Here are a few things to consider in becoming a community of grace.

1
A COMMUNITY OF GRACE WELCOMES ALL

Jesus asks us in Luke 6, "If you love those who love you what credit is that to you?" Is it easy for us to be in community with those we have affinity for but grace allows us to welcome the unwelcome because that's exactly what Christ has done for us. Who is in your margins that you need to invite into community?

2
A COMMUNITY OF GRACE WILL NOT ALLOW US TO PROTECT OUR REPUTATION

When we understand that our identity is in Christ we are free from finding our identity in others' opinions of us. We must be more concerned with God's glory than we are our own reputation. Christ identified himself with a prostitute in the home of a Pharisee. Who are you afraid to invite into your community at the risk of your reputation?

3
A COMMUNITY OF GRACE EXPOSES OUR LEGALISM

When we show a willingness to be vulnerable with people who are different than us it inevitably becomes messy. The sin and brokenness of others will expose the sin and brokenness in our own hearts. Next time you find yourself judging someone in your community for their weirdness, faults, and shortcomings, take a step back and ask yourself why your heart is condemning when you have received such grace. Pray that God would deepen your understanding of his grace and love for you and give you the power to extend that grace and love to your community.

DISTURB US, LORD

Disturb us, Lord, when
We are too well pleased with ourselves,
When our dreams have come true
Because we have dreamed too little,
When we arrived safely
Because we sailed too close to the shore.
Disturb us, Lord, when
With the abundance of things we possess
We have lost our thirst
For the waters of life;
Having fallen in love with life,
We have ceased to dream of eternity
And in our efforts to build a new earth,
We have allowed our vision
Of the new Heaven to dim.
Disturb us, Lord, to dare more boldly,
To venture on wider seas
Where storms will show Your mastery;
Where losing sight of land,
We shall find the stars.
We ask You to push back
The horizons of our hopes;
And to push into the future
In strength, courage, hope, and love.

———

Sir Francis Drake - 1577

being + DOING

An Interview with Pastor Mark Batterson and Tim Willard

WILLARD: Give us your personal theology of technology. Do you have self-imposed restrictions on yourself? Is it different for you as a husband and father than it is as a pastor?

BATTERSON: It's really evolved for me over time. On a macro level, I'm a big believer and proponent that we need to redeem technology and use it for God's purposes. Technology is a wonderful way to save time, it's a wonderful way to keep track and organize your life, but like anything else it can begin to take over.

So over the years there are a few things I've done. When I go on vacation, for example, I try to completely unplug. That means give email a break, give blogging a break.

Right now Twitter is a very interesting technology to me. It seems like you can keep track of what everybody is doing all the time. I love that from the vantage point of a lead pastor with a staff because I follow our staff. It's a way that I can keep track of what they're doing, what they're thinking. I know if someone had a tough night with their baby, or if someone is sick, or if someone saw a movie and they loved it.

So I think that technology, and Twitter in particular, is a great way to be present without being present. The great danger is when you become so consumed that if you're not checking Facebook or Twitter, if you're not checking email, then you feel lazy. It almost becomes an obsessive-compulsive thing for a lot of leaders, because we can't ever not be doing something.

The truth is if you have to always be present then you won't really be present. You need to not be present, and by that I mean Sabbath and rest and check out and guard your day off. If you do that then you can actually be present—be there in the real moment when you need to be.

WILLARD: Some people say that they can't really be in solitude. "I have to have noise around me. I'm just made differently." What do you think of that perspective? Can a person lead a noisy life and truly hear the voice of God?

BATTERSON: No, not according to Psalm 46:10—"Be still and know that I am God." The key part of that is "Be still." If you aren't still, you're going to forget who God is. I think that's a powerful concept.

Let's get down to brass tacks. Most of us don't unplug because we need to be needed. And that's the foible, the Achilles' heel of many leaders. Because of that we stay plugged in because we need to be needed all the time. Eventually you hit a point of diminishing returns. If you try to be everything to everyone, you're going to be nobody to no one.

People have asked me to define the greatest challenge I face in my life right now. My immediate response is margin. Between pastoring a growing church, a growing staff, and then a family with three kids—who are at a stage where they need high investment with their dad—and then writing about a book a year, and traveling and speaking, it is hard to find margin.

If you lose that margin you lose that creativity. I think what happens is that you begin reacting instead of pro-acting. I'm afraid that most people in ministry are just reacting to whatever needs, circumstances, problems, issues are at hand. But you need margin in order to really be proactive and have a vision and lead out of that vision.

WILLARD: Does influence and platform building play into that at all for people who think they need to be plugged in all the time? Is that a real pressure for pastors who want to have influence in our culture? Do you see that as a negative?

BATTERSON: I think that if you're seeking a platform for the wrong reasons, that's a huge problem. I think it's a problem that a lot of leaders fall into. I'd be the first person to confess that there have been times in my life where I've coveted a platform for the wrong reasons. There's no quicker path to spiritual discombobulation than trying to get a platform for the wrong reason.

I think that's something that the Lord gives you in His timing and in His way. It's dangerous to pursue a platform. I think one of the greatest gifts I can give to our congregation is non-availability because my appointments with my heavenly Father take precedence.

I have, for example, two meeting days and two focus days each week. On my meeting days I'll meet with anybody, and I'll try to squeeze in ten to twelve meetings. But I make no apology for having two focus days because if I'm not spending time with God, then the time I spend with you is not going to be very productive.

So I think there's a fine line there, but at the end of the day, when Jesus called His disciples, first and foremost He called them to be *with* Him. The more time you spend with the Lord, and that's in prayer, that's in spiritual discipline, that's in Scripture, then the more productive you're going to be in the time you're going to spend with people.

WILLARD: In *Soul Print* you said that God would like to introduce you to yourself. Why do you think it's so difficult for us to really know who we really are?

BATTERSON: I think it was Blaise Pascal who said, "All of man's misery is derived from his inability to sit quietly by himself in a room alone." We live in a culture where I

IT'S PROBABLY NOT ONE SIMPLE SOLUTION, BUT IF I WAS GOING TO BOIL IT DOWN TO ONE THING, IT WOULD COME BACK TO FINDING A REGULAR ROUTE WHERE IT'S JUST YOU AND GOD. **CALL IT YOUR APPOINTMENT WITH GOD.** IF YOU NEED TO PUT IT ON YOUR CALENDAR, THEN PUT A TIME ON IT AND A PLACE WHERE YOU'RE GOING TO MEET, AND ACTUALLY FORMALIZE IT.

think many people don't want to just be by themselves with themselves because they don't really like what they see or feel. The net result is we really do know more about our favorite celebrities than we do about ourselves. We end up being a stranger to ourselves.

I think that's the byproduct of busyness, that's the byproduct of a lot of white noise in our lives, and that's the challenge of living in a culture where everything happens in real time. That's the challenge of never having to be in a quiet place by yourself.

That's the problem and the question is, *What's the solution?*

It's probably not one simple solution, but if I was going to boil it down to one thing, it would come back to finding a regular route where it's just you and God. Call it your appointment with God. If you need to put it on your calendar, then put a time on it and a place where you're going to meet, and actually formalize it.

I think without that routine then you're never going to get to know yourself, and this is going to sound like a riddle, but if you don't know God you don't know yourself because He knows you better than you know yourself.

Your relationship with God is the key to self-discovery.

WILLARD: Let's talk about that regular time with God. How does prayer factor into your personal walk with Christ. How do *you* pray?

BATTERSON: Well, I just finished my next book *The Circle Maker*, which is book on prayer. Let me answer on a big dream level and then on a personal level.

Fifteen years ago I did a 4.7 mile prayer walk around Capitol Hill. I felt prompted by God to do it. I felt like He had directed me to Joshua 1:3, where God tells Joshua, "I will give you every place where you set your foot" (NIV). But I just felt like God wanted me to stake claim to Capitol Hill. It's a place where God called my family and I felt like He wanted me to claim it as His territory.

So I did a three-hour 4.7 mile prayer walk around Capitol Hill.

Fast forward. God's been answering that prayer for fifteen years. Ebenezer's Coffee House, which we own and operate, was right on that prayer route. It's at 2nd and F streets, NE. It was an absolute miracle how we purchased it. More people offered more money for it than we did; two of them were real estate developers. But we own it.

It was voted the number one coffee house in D.C. But at the end of the day, it's not a coffee house, it's an answered prayer. In the last two years, and I won't get into all the details, but we now own a movie theater. It's a theater dating from 1910-1960 right in the heart of Capitol Hill that we're renovating. We're going to turn it back into a 1930s movie house and it'll be our seventh location. We're doing Sunday morning services there already. I walked right into the marquee fifteen years ago. It was an absolute miracle on how we purchased it.

And then finally, there's an $8 million piece of property that we own that we bought about a year ago. It'll be a future urban campus for us. It was right on the prayer route.

Two years ago I discovered this story of Honi the Circle Maker. It's a true story, found in the Talmud. There was a drought in Israel in the first century B.C., and Honi was famous for praying for rain. So the people asked him to pray for rain, and here's what he did. He took his staff and drew a circle in the sand and he knelt down and said, "Sovereign Lord, I will not leave this circle until You have mercy upon Your children." It was a bold prayer.

He was stuck in the circle if God didn't answer. Long story short, it starts to rain. And he's almost excommunicated by the Sanhedrin because they felt like it was too bold, too demanding, but he ended up being honored for a prayer that saved a generation.

The premise of the book is God honors bold prayers because bold prayers honor God. So I believe that all of the things God has done in National Community Church, if you trace it back to one thing, it's prayer. And not just prayer. One of the things I'm hoping the book reintroduces is the terminology from a generation ago called "praying through." That's where I think a lot of us miss it. We pray, and then we forget what we pray, or we stop praying.

But *The Circle Maker* is about circling the promises of God, circling the dreams He's given us, circling our kids, circling pieces of property, and you just keep praying around them much like the Israelites marched around the city of Jericho. You're going to keep circling that thing because you believe God wants it for you. At the end of the day, prayer is right at the heart of everything we're about and everything that God's done. That's kind of the macro answer.

On a personal level, let me get practical since that was a historical, philosophical answer. I love this story about Daniel where it says three times a day he would go upstairs and kneel down to pray in front of an open window facing Jerusalem. How curious is that? It's such a detailed description.

What I love about it was he had a place to go and pray. It was a place where, when he went there, he was in prayer mode. So one thing that's important is having a place to pray. And of course, Jesus talked about having a prayer closet. For me, I pop the latch, climb the ladder, and get up on the rooftop at Ebenezer's Coffee House. When I need to "pray through," that's where I pray. I pace back and forth. I love praying there because I'm praying on top of an answered prayer, so it's hard not to have faith when I'm up on that rooftop.

So, my admonition to leaders is you need to find a place where you get good reception, a place where you can focus, a place where you feel like you have the faith to pray through. For Daniel it was praying through a window. You've got to find that place where you can dial in and you can pray through. There is no substitute.

Nothing can take the place of that. If you don't "pray through," then I'm not buying your stock. That's my exhortation for the day.

WILLARD: Frederick Buechner says, "The place God calls you to is where your deep gladness and the world's deep hunger meet." How does being present to what is going on around us factor into the discovery of our calling?

BATTERSON: That's one of my favorite Buechner quotes. He says, "Listen to the voice of gladness." Maybe this would be a decent landing strip because I think it's one of the big lessons I learned.

When I first started pastoring there were about 20-25 people. It was a rag-tag group. I didn't even feel like a pastor yet. The church didn't feel like a church. The first few years were really tough. And I think I fell into what I've since termed the "when/then" syndrome. *When* this happens or *when* that happens, *when* I get married, *when* we have kids, *when* I retire, or *when* the church is a thousand people, it's when/then.

Truthfully? If you can't be happy in the here and now, you're not going to experience joy then and there. One of the things I think the Lord spoke to me in those early years was enjoy the journey. I think the key to enjoying the journey is to be present.

Here's what I know about leaders. True leaders are visionaries, and visionaries dream of the future. But the great challenge is you still have to be present. You still have to be in the moment and enjoy where you are right here right now, because if you don't learn how to do that right here right now, I promise you won't learn to do it then and there. It's like the person who says, "Once I start making more money I'll start tithing." No you won't. You won't. Because if you can't do it with a small amount you're not going to do it with a large amount.

You just need to enjoy the journey and be present in the moment. Hopefully there's something there out of my experience, and I'm still learning that. You never arrive. I've learned that as a pastor, as a writer. You can't wait until this book hits the *New York Times* or this church has this many locations. You know, it's a lie. The sooner you can identify that as a lie and be in the moment and enjoy the journey, the more God is going to be glorified in you and through you. ◨

PSALM 84

How lovely is your dwelling place,
O LORD of hosts!
My soul longs, yes, faints
for the courts of the LORD;
my heart and flesh sing for joy
to the living God.

Even the sparrow finds a home,
and the swallow a nest for herself,
where she may lay her young,
at your altars, O LORD of hosts,
my King and my God.
Blessed are those who dwell in your house,
ever singing your praise!
Selah

Blessed are those whose strength is in you,
in whose heart are the highways to Zion.
As they go through the Valley of Baca
they make it a place of springs;
the early rain also covers it with pools.
They go from strength to strength;
each one appears before God in Zion.

O LORD God of hosts, hear my prayer;
give ear, O God of Jacob!
Selah
(ESV)

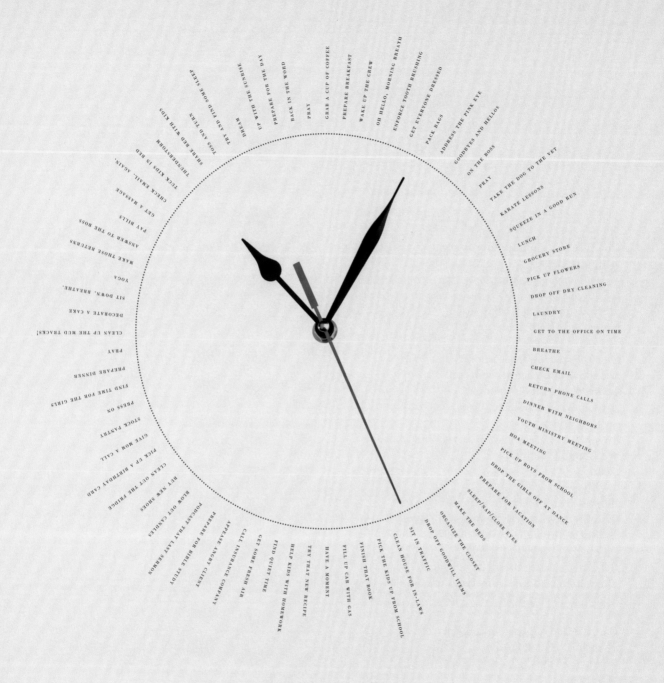

chasing the
UTOPIAN "ALL"

Christine Caine

It can be difficult in our fast-paced, multi-option, ever-changing, communication frenzied world to actually be *present* in *all* that we do. Sometimes I think the more we load up our plate, the less of it we actually partake. Are we chasing a utopian "all"—trying to do more, but actually truly engaging less?

Think about it. We are constantly told that we can have it all, be it all, and do it all. So we pursue this "all." I often attempt to roll up my sleeves, in true "Rosie the Riveter" style (to reveal my femininely chiseled arms, of course—ha!), and belt out the lyrics to "I Am Woman Hear Me Roar" in my best Helen Reddy voice. My mission: to accomplish more in one day than the Proverbs 31 woman.

Let's admit it ladies, we've all done it, haven't we?

We get up an hour early to exercise, another hour earlier to pray, and a third hour is needed to get the kids ready and packed for school. We are consummate organizers, jugglers, and problem solvers as we manage our spouse, children, church commitments, friendships, finances, groceries, mealtimes, our kid's extra-curricular activities, quiet time with God, and whatever else is on the agenda. Then, at the end of the day we stay up an hour longer to ensure the house is clean, an additional hour to read a chapter of the latest bestseller, and one more hour to ensure we spend "quality time" with our spouse. It almost gets to the point that we should forego sleep altogether because the moment our head touches the pillow, it's time to rise and shine.

We've set out on this mission to do it "all" only to discover that in order to achieve it, we need an extra 24 hours in every day. Even worse, we aren't even really present in the hours that we do have because we are so busy thinking about what we have to accomplish next.

DISAPPOINTMENT AND FULFILLMENT

The fact is that the pursuit of having and doing it all has left many of us disappointed, discouraged, exhausted, defeated, anxious, stressed, and unable to enjoy any of what we "have." Despite our sometimes superhuman exploits, we begin to question the pace and fullness of this "having and doing it all" life and whether or not we have all been sold a big lie. In our disillusionment, we can even begin to think there is no possible way we can manage a strong Christian walk, an amazing marriage, great kids, a fulfilling sex life, fantastic friends, and pursuing our God-given purpose.

The truth is, you *can* have it all, and you *can* do it all. Our problem is that we carry an incorrect perception of what the "all" is. We are then left feeling like we fall short and are unable to actually be truly present in any of it. If we want to live well and fulfill the purpose God has for our lives then we need to discover His definition of the "all" and pursue that.

When I was a teenager, I wanted to be a basketball player. Then the reality hit: the statistical probability of a petite 5'2" girl making headlines because of her ability to slam-dunk a basketball was next to nothing. If I had chosen to ignore this fact and equated my "all" with being the next WNBA superstar, I would have wasted many years in a futile pursuit. The point is that each one of us has a specific "all" created especially for us, and if we pursue only this, God in turn enables us to achieve it.

Having it all has nothing to do with our own fleshly desires. And it certainly has nothing to do with what the culture tells us our life dreams should be. Rather, having it all should be the result of seeking first the Kingdom of God—*His all.*

HIS ALL

In Matthew 6:33, Jesus says, "But seek first the kingdom of God and his righteousness, and all these things will be added to you." (ESV) When it's God who adds the "all" rather than us trying to strive for it on our own, our perspective changes. The stress that accompanies pursuing the world's all falls away. If we simply continue to put God first, He adds it to our life according to His perfect will and His perfect timing.

Similarly, the Bible teaches that there are certain things God has created for each one of us to do. The book of Ephesians says, "For we are God's [own] handiwork (His workmanship), recreated in Christ Jesus, [born anew] that we may do those good works which God predestined (planned beforehand) for us [taking paths which He prepared ahead of time], that we should walk in them [living the good life which He prearranged and made ready for us to live]." (Ephesians 2:10 AMP)

If we spend our lives doing the good works God already planned for us, we will always find enough time, energy, and resources to do it all—and we will be able to be present for all of it. On the other hand, if we try to walk in paths God has not prepared for us, doing works He has not set out for us, we will inevitably end up living stressed, unfulfilled, frustrated, disappointed, and unable to enjoy what we "have" because our minds are too focused on what we have to do next.

The "all" we should want to have and do is tied in to God Himself and His purpose for our lives. If we seek Him first always and align our lives with the good works He has prepared for us to do, it is truly amazing how our crazy, full-to-overflowing lives seem to work. **C**

This excerpt was taken from Christine's new book, *Can I Have (and do) It All, Please?* Used with permission. Published by Equip & Empower Ministries.

HAVING IT ALL HAS NOTHING TO DO WITH OUR OWN FLESHLY DESIRES. AND IT CERTAINLY HAS NOTHING TO DO WITH WHAT THE CULTURE TELLS US OUR LIFE DREAMS SHOULD BE. RATHER, HAVING IT ALL SHOULD BE THE RESULT OF SEEKING FIRST THE KINGDOM OF GOD—

HIS ALL.

*BACK TO LIFE

Andy Stanley

Everything we experience is processed through our hearts, the good and the bad. Life comes at us from all directions, but it all gets channeled through our hearts. Unfortunately, our negative experiences have a tendency to get stuck there. Eventually they make their way out through our words and deeds; but because of the delay between entry and exit, we often have a difficult time making the connection.

So we're mad and discontent but don't know why. We're resentful toward certain types of people, though they've done nothing to deserve it. We're jealous even though we know it's foolish to dislike somebody for having something we don't. These things make no sense, but they're real. Left unchecked they can drive us into self-destructive and relationship-wrecking behavior patterns.

So maybe Jesus was right. Maybe all that junk we don't like about ourselves really does come "from the heart."

HURT RUNS DEEP

Unresolved hurt runs deep. So deep, in fact, I have seen it erase some people's faith in God. They no longer believe in a personal God—not for theological reasons, but because they can't get past what happened to them or someone they loved. And if you were to hear their stories, you would understand. If they were to hear *your* story, they would probably understand your dilemma as well. Life can take the legs right out from under our faith.

I've gotten to the point that when I meet somebody who's really down on the church and/or God, I rarely engage them in a theological conversation. Theology isn't what drove them to their ... theology. Nine times out of ten, it was a life experience or a series of experiences that left something distorted in their hearts. And over time, this something eroded their faith in God. Again, Jesus' words come to mind, "From the heart comes ..." and we can fill in the blank.

On many occasions I've seen people's faith spring back to life, seemingly overnight, once they began to address their heart issues. That's exactly what happened with Joe. I met Joe at Starbucks. He was sitting in one of those overstuffed chairs with headphones on and a scowl that said, "Don't anybody come near me." If the expression on his face wasn't enough, Joe was about fifty-five years old and not a small fellow. Everything about his countenance and posture communicated anger. So when I saw him I avoided eye contact and went on about my business.

ON MANY OCCASIONS I'VE SEEN PEOPLE'S FAITH SPRING BACK TO LIFE, SEEMINGLY OVERNIGHT, ONCE THEY BEGAN TO ADDRESS THEIR HEART ISSUES.

*

As I was waiting for my soy latte, Joe approached me and said, "Aren't you Andy?" At that particular moment I wasn't sure if I should be Andy or not. From the look on his face, I knew I didn't want to be me. But because there were plenty of people around to witness whatever was about to happen, I nodded.

"Somebody gave me one of your CDs," he said. "I've been listening to it. But I've got to tell you, I have a real problem with God, and the church too, for that matter."

Joe had been through two difficult divorces. His first wife had been sexually abused as a child and was never able to face the issues involved. After thirty years of marriage, the memories of abuse surfaced and eroded their marriage, which ended in divorce. His ex-wife passed away suddenly two years later. Joe then remarried, but after three years this too ended in a heartbreaking divorce. Joe was lonely, a recovering alcoholic. There was no evidence of the existence of God, as far as he could see.

I wasn't sure what to say, so I asked him if he would be willing to read a book. He said he would. I told him to buy Philip Yancey's *Disappointment with God*, but I honestly didn't think he would.

FIXING THE RATTLE

I never expected to see Joe again. But I did.

A couple of weeks later, there he was, sitting in the same chair at Starbucks. This time, no headphones. I remembered his face but not his name. He walked up to me and said, "I read that book." For a minute I couldn't remember what book he was talking about.

Halfway through the conversation I mustered the courage to ask him to remind me of his name. He didn't seem offended. The book hadn't really helped, he told me, but it really was a great book.

So I said, "Joe, would you be willing to talk to someone?" He hesitated. "I don't think it's going to do any good," he said.

I wasn't sure it would either, but I did know that Joe needed help. And I knew just the person who could help him. I got Joe's phone number and connected him with one of our pastors, John Woodall. John called Joe, met him for coffee, and struck up a friendship. That was the last I saw of Joe, for a while.

Three months later I was sitting in that same Starbucks, talking to a student pastor from another church, when

in walked Joe. When he saw me he headed straight for my table. The first thing I noticed was that he was smiling. The second thing I noticed was that he was carrying a Bible, a notebook, and a book on marriage.

"I'm getting remarried next week!" he announced. I wasn't sure what to think.

"To who?" I asked.

"To Susan!" he exclaimed. Susan was his ex-wife.

"Susan and I are getting remarried. John is doing the wedding."

I could see in Joe's eyes that something remarkable had happened. And it had. Over the course of several meetings with John, Joe found the courage to quit blaming and instead take a look at what was rattling around in his heart. He'd been an angry man, with reason to be angry. But like so many people, Joe had no idea what to *do* about his anger. And his unresolved anger had eroded his faith to the point where it was almost nonexistent.

John had helped Joe to embrace a new habit to replace his anger and immediately, Joe's faith had come to life. With his renewed faith came the motivation he needed to address other issues in his life. The transformation was so remarkable that Susan noticed and began asking questions. Soon after, she put her faith in Christ. The week before Susan and Joe were remarried, John baptized her in one of our morning services.

Joe's story reminds me of lyrics from the Evanescence tune "Bring Me to Life":

> *Where I've become so numb without a soul, ...*
> *Until you find it there and lead it back home.*

Like so many, Joe had become numb to the life of God because of damage to his heart. To his credit, Joe had the courage to ask for help. His heavenly Father was eager to respond and brought Joe back to life. ▣

REFLECTION

Can your hidden scars end up becoming a matter of integrity? Of course they can. That was certainly the case with Joe. His unresolved problems with anger led to him divorcing his wife. Our integrity as leaders reflects our wholeness as a person. But more importantly it reflects our wholeness in Christ.

Andy challenges us to be courageous enough to confront the deep matters affecting our heart; matters that ultimately affect how we lead others, how we communicate with others, and how we love others. With Andy's challenge in mind, take a few quiet moments to consider the following:

1
WHAT'S YOUR COMMUNITY SAYING?

Ask a few of your closest friends out to coffee at different times. Use that time to ask your friend to be candid with you regarding anything he or she has observed over the years or months that might be cause for concern. Is there a pattern of abusive talk or extreme negativity in your life? Perhaps you have already pinpointed something within that is troubling you. If so, ask them if they see it as well. Do they confirm your notion? Ask them to pray for you in this area. Ask if it's okay if you talk to them about it from time to time.

2
WHAT'S YOUR SPOUSE SAYING?

If you don't have a spouse but have a significant other, then substitute. Our spouses (and significant others) have the best seat in the house regarding our habits and inclinations. Humbly ask them to assess a course of behavior that they find troubling or out of the ordinary. Again, if you have a grasp on what it is, ask them to pray with you about it and seek ways to take further steps to heal the heart wound.

3
WHAT IS YOUR SOUL SAYING?

This question is a set up. If you feel like you're numb to the world then you know what your soul is saying. It needs healing! But there is more to inner healing than the typical spiritual standby answers. Your soul and body are connected. You are a whole being. As you seek to nourish your inner self, spend some time replenishing your body as well. Shake up your routine and get outside. Get back on that exercise regimen you started on January 1. Getting physically active is not going to solve your problem. It will, however, help to clear the cobwebs in your mind and heart and help you see more clearly what needs to happen in order for you to find healing.

CONTEMPLATIVE ACTIVISM:

A TRANSFORMATIVE WAY

PHILEENA HEUERTZ

We are complex human beings created in the image of God—daughters and sons of the most high God. We are the beloved of God. This is an extraordinary identity. But we don't often reflect this heritage. Instead of living from a place of knowing in our core that we are loved, which fuels our ability to love God with our whole being while loving others, we live at a lower level of awareness. In some cases we become too egocentric. In other cases we think too poorly of ourselves.

The human condition is anchored in our search for God and for ourselves—to know and be known. When we awaken to the spiritual journey, we find that surrender and letting go are the surest of ways to find out who we truly are, who God is, and who our neighbor is. The spiritual journey invites us to come into fuller understanding and acceptance of our belovedness so that we can love others and become co-creators with God.

Fr. Thomas Keating, a seasoned Cistercian monk, promotes contemplative prayer as a way to surrender to Christian transformation. In his book *The Human Condition: Contemplation and Transformation,* Keating offers contemporary wisdom by identifying three emotional "programs for happiness." If we're honest, we can find ourselves interacting with the world primarily through one of these three "programs":

» Power and Control
» Affection and Esteem
» Security and Survival

Keating says these three "programs for happiness" emerge from basic instinctual needs. It's a natural part of our human development to seek a degree of power and control, affection and esteem, and security and survival. In time, however, we over-identify with one by way of compensating for that basic need which may have gone largely unmet in our childhood; thus, the false self gains fuel for its existence. Essentially our "program for happiness" becomes the archetype of our false self.

As we grow in self-awareness we often realize that some of our reactions to present circumstances are actually reactions to past events that are buried in our unconscious. Self-awareness is a central aspect to the Christian life. Self-knowledge paves the way to becoming whole and connected to God and others.

A first step toward self-awareness is recognizing the immanent (all pervasive presence) as well as transcendent

ACTION WITHOUT CONTEMPLATION CAN BE A DANGEROUS ROAD—LEAVING US BLIND TO THE PITFALLS OF THE MOTIVATIONS OF OUR FALSE SELF.

(independent of the created world) nature of God. The Christian doctrine of the Divine indwelling affirms God's immanence—we believe that God dwells in our soul.

It seems, however, we relate more often to God's transcendence without affirming God's immanence. When we don't hold God's immanence and transcendence in tension or balance, our sense that God is distant from us—somewhere out there—can increase relational distance between God and us.

A lack of experience of God's indwelling presence further propagates the notion that God is looking down on us, keeping a check-list of our right and wrong behavior. The burden of living the Christian life then falls on me to do and behave appropriately. The task can become burdensome and dreadful—far from the abundant life Jesus invited us into. We need a spiritual revolution like the Apostle Paul wrote about in Ephesians:

> ... *Your mind must be renewed by a spiritual revolution, so that you can put on the new self that has been created in God's likeness, in the justice and holiness of the truth.*[2]

This kind of revolution starts with a commitment to "know thyself."[3] For a transformational revolution to take place in our lives, we must submit to a spiritual journey marked by contemplation *and* action.

CULTIVATING CONTEMPLATION

It seems that few of us struggle with being active enough. The more common theme I notice is that of struggling to know what to say "no" to and how to live a simpler life. We are very active people and some might argue we are over-active. While some of our actions may be cloaked in the name of righteousness and justice, or in the name of "loving our neighbor," other actions are rooted in selfishness or at least short-sightedness.

While our behavior, conduct, initiative, and enterprise can be well-meaning and good intentioned, many of our best good acts are not good enough. And some of our well-meaning intentions even cause more harm than good. Time and time again, action without contemplation leads us off course in the journey of life.

Contemplation affirms our need for a spiritual revolution. It reminds us that God is God and "I" am not. A lifestyle of contemplation fosters personal and communal transformation.

I understand contemplation, in its broad sense, to mean creating sacred space to be still, to rest in God, to reflect, to look inward; to attend to the inner life; to simply be with God in solitude, silence, and stillness. Solitude, silence, and stillness are, in fact, the qualities of contemplative prayer.

So how do we cultivate contemplation?

It takes discipline. Contemplative prayer practices are more to us like disciplines than prayer as we've been accustomed to understand it. That's because the dominant type of prayer that has been taught in modern Western Christianity is cataphatic prayer—prayer that makes use of our faculties (reason, imagination, memory, feelings, and will). Cataphatic prayer corresponds with ordinary awareness and our ego.

By contrast, apophatic prayer does not make use of our normal faculties but transcends them. The center of orientation for this kind of prayer—by its very nature—is not "I" but abandonment of self and attentiveness to God. But this prayer does make use of different kinds of faculties, faculties that we are less in touch with, faculties known as "spiritual senses."[4]

Contemplative prayer starts from the orientation that we need to receive from God. Contemplative practices teach us how to surrender to the presence and action of God within us *and* within our world. The fruit of contemplative prayer is not looked for or found during the prayer time. The contemplative space that we allow to be cultivated by the Holy Spirit within us over time, produces a garden of abundant fruit in our active life— fruit produced by the Master Gardener.

A TRANSFORMATIVE WAY: CONTEMPLATIVE ACTIVISM

Action without contemplation can be a dangerous road—leaving us blind to the pitfalls of the motivations of our false self. Action without contemplation doesn't allow for the space and awareness needed to let God introduce God's self to us—free of preconceived notions and biased filters.

A life of action without contemplation is characterized by:
» Activism instead of acts of love
» Criticizing without energizing
» Despair instead of hope
» Disconnection between "doing" and "being"
» Fundamentalism and judgmentalism

Action without contemplation is not an obedient life and appears rather absurd when we honestly examine it. Without contemplation, the liberation and fecund life of which Jesus taught is out of reach, and his admonition that we would do even greater things than he seems impossible.

Contemplation leads to just and compassionate action, and action born from the heart of God leads to contemplation. A commitment to contemplation leads to radical action. Contemplative activism makes us supple in the hands of God. By way of Christ's ongoing, transformative work in us, we are able to love and serve more freely, purely, and unconditionally—like Jesus.

In a world that is plagued by human exploitation, violence, and destruction of our ecosphere, we owe it to the world to develop contemplative activism. ◼

---

[1] The "false self" term is generally attributed to Thomas Merton who encapsulated the "true self" and "false self" in reference to the Apostle Paul's teaching on the old and new creation.

[2] Ephesians 4:17-18, 20-24 TLB

[3] Socrates' guiding philosophical rule that holds both spiritual and practical wisdom

[4] For more exploration of cataphatic and apophatic prayer, see Cynthia Bourgeault's book *Centering Prayer and Inner Awakening* (Cambridge, Mass.: Cowley, 2004), chap. 4.

This article originally appeared in the Fall 2010 issue of *Conversations Journal*, "Contemplation and Action" vol.8.2, pp. 46-51. It is reprinted here with permission from the publisher. http://conversationsjournal.com

radical TOGETHER

An Interview with Pastor David Platt and Ken Coleman

COLEMAN: David, you've got a follow-up book to *Radical* called *Radical Together*. Tell us what's going on with this book.

PLATT: *Radical* was about what it really means to follow the Jesus of the Bible in our culture. So *Radical Together* basically takes that a step deeper and says if this is what it means to follow Jesus, how does that affect how we gather as a community of faith, and what we do as a community in the church. The reality is that none of us is intended to live out radical obedience to Christ on our own. We'll only advance the kingdom when we are doing that together. The book is some foundational truths and ideas that are born out of what we've been walking through at our church and what God is doing in the context of His people around the world.

COLEMAN: What did God teach you as you were writing the book?

PLATT: As I was writing the second book, I was solidifying those things God was putting in my heart. At the same time, it was like I was in over my head with lots still to learn. I remember thinking that the ramifications of this go even farther than what I've even yet to experience and what our church is yet to experience.

COLEMAN: What has happened since *Radical* came out, in your church and in your own community? Can you tell us any stories you're hearing from around the world as a result of the book and the ideas that you put forward?

PLATT: In our church, it's been really exciting to see the different stories. We've had numerous families pack their bags in the suburbs and move to lower income inner-city areas in Birmingham to live out the gospel there. We just sent out a family that's leading a team into one of the most dangerous people groups in the world. There are all kinds of families that are adopting and doing foster care, that are just saying, "Okay, instead of spending our resources and our time focused on what the culture says is important, how can we redeem all of that and focus on the advancement of the gospel?"

It has also been exciting to see it multiply in all different contexts. So it may be a traditional church in the Southeast that's really taking a look at things and asking some questions that really need to be asked, or church plants in the Northeast or Northwest setting the vision for the very beginning of planting churches, to talking to brothers and sisters in other contexts around the world.

COLEMAN: You mentioned adoption and foster care. At Catalyst, we've been very intentional through all of our events and through social media to promote this issue. So I want you to share with our audience how adoption has entered into your world and where you're at on the journey.

PLATT: My wife and I, for about five years, wanted to have children. So this adoption process began as kind of a real struggle. We wanted to have children, so why was God not giving us children? If I'm honest, I viewed adoption kind of like a second best; but we learned very quickly that this is not second best. This is best, and what a great picture of the gospel!

We adopted our first son, Caleb, from Kazakhstan. We ended up having our second son in the natural way.

And we're now in the process of two more adoptions: one from Nepal and one from China.

Adoption has been great in our own family, and then to see this picture of adoption play out in the church and in our community of faith has been really exciting. We've got tons of families adopting domestically and internationally, and we've had a big emphasis on foster care. We were studying through James, and came upon James 1:27, and saw God's priority for the care of the orphans. We called the Department of Human Resources in our county and asked them if they had any needs for caring for orphans and children in our county. They laughed and said they have tons of needs. I asked, "If there was a miracle, how many families would it take to cover all the needs that you have?" They said, "We could use 150 more families." So we challenged the church, and 160 families signed up to do foster care and adoption. Our community of faith wants to show the love of the Father to the fatherless in the context of the county we live in.

COLEMAN: We all have different journeys, David, as you know, in how we view God early on. At some point, that's stripped away and you just experience God in a very real way. How has adoption changed you? You're a pastor. How has it changed the way you view God, or what has it taught you about God?

PLATT: J. I. Packer said our level of understanding of what it means to be a Christian is really determined by how much we make of having God as our Father and us being a child. So to see that in a whole new light, as a result of this journey of adoption, the view of God as our Father comes alive in a whole new way. Every mention of God as Father, especially in the New Testament, and every mention of us as His sons and daughters or His children shows us a beautiful picture of the gospel. It's just the reality that He sought after me when there was nothing in me worth seeking after, and He sought me and loved me while everything in me was rebelling against Him.

This picture of God has been key in our own family and in my own life, and also in these other families who are adopting and doing foster care. One of the things I try to emphasize in our church when it comes to this issue

EVERY MENTION OF GOD AS FATHER, ESPECIALLY IN THE NEW TESTAMENT, AND **EVERY MENTION OF US AS HIS SONS AND DAUGHTERS OR HIS CHILDREN SHOWS US A BEAUTIFUL PICTURE OF THE GOSPEL.** IT'S JUST THE REALITY THAT HE SOUGHT AFTER ME WHEN THERE WAS NOTHING IN ME WORTH SEEKING AFTER, AND HE SOUGHT ME AND LOVED ME WHILE EVERYTHING IN ME WAS REBELLING AGAINST HIM.

of adoption and foster care is that it's not necessarily easy. Our adoption process was pretty smooth, but there are a lot of families in our church right now who are in the process of adoption and foster care who have come upon some very rough circumstances. They have brought kids into their homes, who, to be honest, are dangerous to their other children because of some of the circumstances that some of these kids have grown up in. And so what I've tried to emphasize is that this is not just a case of trying to have a nice cute Christmas card to send out. This is the gospel that drives us, and it's the only thing that's going to sustain us when we have a child in our home who is a physical threat to our other children. How can you continue to love a child who may be in a situation where they resist your love toward them every time? I think the gospel alone is going to sustain us in those times, not the vision of the cute Christmas card. It's the reality of the gospel that God on high looked at us in our rebellion against Him, and when we were resisting every bit of love and every manifestation of it that was shown to us, He still pursued us. That's what's going to motivate mom and dad to continue to persevere in love to a child who's gone through some rough things in life.

COLEMAN: I want you to address a real perception that exists. And that is, if you're considering adoption, this idea that "I've got biological children, and I may love them more" nonsense. But I want you to speak to that out of your adoption experiences because it's a very real perception.

PLATT: I think it is fear of the unknown. We have this tendency to think we can only love a physical child in this way. But this undercuts the gospel. We have indescribable love for both of our boys that we could never have imagined. And even that is spiritual at the core, it's gospel at the core, because we are spiritual children with God. We think of family in terms of bloodline more than relationship and affection, but we are adopted into the family of God. He has brought us into His family.

COLEMAN: David, please share what God is teaching you and your staff, your team, right now. What's challenging you? What are you excited about?

PLATT: I think the big thing is how we as leaders can create a culture in the church that is not dependent on us, but where we are empowering people to do the work of ministry. Instead of us organizing programs for the people in order to have ministry accomplished, let's equip people for ministry. Let's serve them, let's empower them, let's send them out, let's give the responsibility for the advancement of the kingdom to the whole body, and in the process, unleash the people of God for the purpose of God. If all 4,500 people who attend Brook Hills go out in the Spirit of God to accomplish the mission of God, the gates of hell can't stop the spread of the gospel in Birmingham and to the ends of the earth.

COLEMAN: Who are the leaders or people from history that you greatly admire?

PLATT: Missionary biographies have had the most influence on me. It's those men and women who have been willing to pioneer and step out into realms that were not popular that nobody had gone into before, like Jim Elliot, Adoniram Judson, and David Livingstone. And I think of pastors like Charles Spurgeon, who was a pastor who loved people, who wanted to lead people to Christ, who had solid theology, and who toiled and worked hard. I want those things, those traits, to be evident in my life.

COLEMAN: If you could gather every young church leader and give them just one message from your heart, your thoughts, what you're learning, what would you share with them?

PLATT: The most important thing is our personal intimacy with Christ. If that's not there, then no matter how successful we might be even in church culture, we're missing the point. I encourage every leader to consider how we regard our first love. Christ would have our affections and our hearts. And everything we do, with our different gifts and skills, in the different positions we find ourselves, that it would all flow out of our intimacy with Christ. ▣

PSALM 139

God, investigate my life; get all the facts firsthand.
I'm an open book to you;
even from a distance, you know what I'm thinking.
You know when I leave and when I get back;
I'm never out of your sight.
You know everything I'm going to say
before I start the first sentence.
I look behind me and you're there,
then up ahead and you're there, too—
your reassuring presence, coming and going.
This is too much, too wonderful—
I can't take it all in!

Is there anyplace I can go to avoid your Spirit?
to be out of your sight?
If I climb to the sky, you're there!
If I go underground, you're there!
If I flew on morning's wings
to the far western horizon,
You'd find me in a minute—
you're already there waiting!
Then I said to myself, "Oh, he even sees me in the dark!
At night I'm immersed in the light!"
It's a fact: darkness isn't dark to you;
night and day, darkness and light, they're all the same
to you.

Oh yes, you shaped me first inside, then out;
you formed me in my mother's womb.
I thank you, High God—you're breathtaking!
Body and soul, I am marvelously made!
I worship in adoration—what a creation!
You know me inside and out,
you know every bone in my body;
You know exactly how I was made, bit by bit,
how I was sculpted from nothing into something.
Like an open book, you watched me grow from con-
ception to birth;
all the stages of my life were spread out before you,
The days of my life all prepared
before I'd even lived one day.

Your thoughts—how rare, how beautiful!
God, I'll never comprehend them!
I couldn't even begin to count them—
any more than I could count the sand of the sea.
Oh, let me rise in the morning and live always with you!
And please, God, do away with wickedness for good!
And you murderers—out of here!—
all the men and women who belittle you, God,
infatuated with cheap god-imitations.
See how I hate those who hate you, God,
see how I loathe all this godless arrogance;
I hate it with pure, unadulterated hatred.
Your enemies are my enemies!

Investigate my life, O God,
find out everything about me;
Cross-examine and test me,
get a clear picture of what I'm about;
See for yourself whether I've done anything wrong—
then guide me on the road to eternal life.
(MSG)

THE
extinction
OF SACRED SPACE

Scott Belsky

Interruption-free space is sacred. Yet, in the digital era we live in, we are losing hold of the few sacred spaces that remain untouched by email, the Internet, people, and other forms of distraction. Our cars now have mobile phone integration and a thousand satellite radio stations. When walking from one place to another, we have our devices streaming data from dozens of sources. Even at our bedside, we now have our iPads with heaps of digital apps and the world's information at our fingertips.

There has been much discussion about the value of the "creative pause"—a state described as "the shift from being fully engaged in a creative activity to being passively engaged, or the shift to being disengaged altogether." This phenomenon is the seed of the breakthrough "aha!" moments that people so frequently report having in the shower. In these moments, you are completely isolated, and your mind is able to wander and churn big questions without interruption.

However, despite the incredible power and potential of sacred spaces, they are quickly becoming extinct. We are depriving ourselves of every opportunity for disconnection. And our imaginations suffer the consequences.

WHY DO WE CRAVE DISTRACTION OVER DOWNTIME?

Why do we give up our sacred space so easily? Because space is scary. During these temporary voids of distraction, our minds return to the uncertainty and fears that plague all of us. To escape this chasm of self-doubt and unanswered questions, you tune into all of the activity and data for reassurance.

But this desperate need for constant connection and stimulation is not a modern problem. I would argue that we have always sought a state of constant connection from the dawn of time, it's just never been possible until now.

The need to be connected is, in fact, very basic in Maslow's hierarchy of needs, the psychological theory that explains the largest and most fundamental human desires. Our need for a sense of belonging comes right after physical safety. We thrive on friendship, family, and the constant affirmation of our existence and relevance. Our self-esteem is largely a product of our interactions with others.

It is now possible to always feel loved and cared for, thanks to the efficiency of our "comment walls" on

Facebook and seamless connection with everyone we've ever known. Your confidence and self-esteem can quickly be reassured by checking your number of "followers" on Twitter or the number of "likes" garnered by your photographs and blog posts. The traction you are getting in your projects, or with your business, can now be measured and reported in real time.

Our insatiable need to tune into information—at the expense of savoring our downtime—is a form of "work" (something I call "insecurity work") that we do to reassure ourselves.

SO WHAT'S THE SOLUTION? HOW DO WE RECLAIM OUR SACRED SPACES?

Soon enough, planes, trains, subways and yes, even showers will offer the option of staying connected. Knowing that we cannot rely on spaces that force us to unplug to survive much longer, we must be proactive in creating these spaces for ourselves. And when we have a precious opportunity to *not* be connected, we should develop the capacity to use it and protect it.

Here are five potential mindsets and solutions for consideration:

I. RITUALS FOR UNPLUGGING.

The notion of a day every week reserved for reflection has become more important than ever before. It's about more than just refraining from work. It's about unplugging. The recent Sabbath Manifesto movement has received mainstream secular accolades for the concept of ritualizing the period of disconnection. Perhaps you will reserve one day on the weekend where you force yourself to disconnect. At first, such efforts will feel very uncomfortable. You will deal with a bout of "connection withdrawal," but stay with it.

2. DAILY DOSES OF DEEP THINKING.

Perhaps "sacred space" is a new life tenet that we must adopt in the 21st century. Since we know that unplugging will only become more difficult over time, we will need to develop a discipline for ourselves. Back in the day when the TV became a staple of every American home, parents started mandating time for their children to read. "TV time" became a controlled endeavor

because, otherwise, it would consume every waking moment. Now, every waking moment is "connected time," and we need to start controlling it.

We need some rules. When it comes to scheduling, we will need to allocate blocks of time for deep thinking. Maybe you will carve out a one-to-two hour block on your calendar every day for taking a walk or grabbing a cup of coffee and just pondering some of those bigger things. I can even imagine a day when homes and apartments have a special switch that shuts down wi-fi and data access during dinner or at night—just to provide a temporary pause from the constant flow of status updates and other communications.

3. MEDITATION AND NAPS TO CLEAR THE MIND.

There is no better mental escape from our tech-charged world than the act of meditation. If only for fifteen minutes, the ability to steer your mind away from constant stimulation is downright liberating. There are various kinds of meditation. Some forms require you to think about nothing and completely clear your mind. (This is quite hard, at least for me.) Other forms of meditation are about focusing on one specific thing—often your breath, or a mantra that you repeat in your head (or out loud) for ten to fifteen minutes. At first, any sort of meditation will feel like a chore. But with practice, it will become an energizing exercise.

If you can't adopt meditation, you might also try clearing your mind the old-fashioned way—by sleeping. The legendary energy expert and bestselling author Tony Schwartz takes a twenty-minute nap every day. Even if it's a few hours before he presents to a packed audience, he'll take a short nap. I asked him how he overcomes the midday anxiety enough to nap. His trick? "Practice," he said. Like all skills that don't come naturally, practice makes perfect.

4. SELF-AWARENESS AND PSYCHOLOGICAL INVESTMENT.

Our most basic fears and desires, both conscious and subconscious, are soothed by connectivity and a constant flow of information. It is supremely important that we recognize the power of our insecurities and, at the very least,

THE POTENTIAL OF OUR OWN CREATIVITY IS RAP-
IDLY BEING COMPROMISED BY THE ERA WE LIVE
IN. I BELIEVE THAT GENIUS IN THE 21ST CENTURY
WILL BE ATTRIBUTED TO PEOPLE WHO ARE ABLE TO
UNPLUG FROM THE CONSTANT STATE OF "REAC-
TIONARY WORKFLOW," REDUCE THEIR AMOUNT
OF INSECURITY WORK, AND ALLOW THEIR MINDS
TO SOLVE THE GREAT CHALLENGES OF OUR ERA.

acknowledge where our anxiety comes from. Awareness is always the first step in solving any problem.

During research for my book, *Making Ideas Happen*, I was surprised by how many legendary creative leaders credited some form of therapy as a part of their professional success. If you're willing to invest in it, then take the plunge. Whatever you learn will help you understand your fears and the actions you take as a result.

5. PROTECT THE STATE OF NO–INTENT.
When you're rushing to a solution, your mind will jump to the easiest and most familiar path. But when you allow yourself to just look out the window for ten minutes—and ponder—your brain will start working in a more creative way. It will grasp ideas from unexpected places. It's this very sort of unconscious creativity that

leads to great thinking. When you're driving or showering, you're letting your mind wander because you don't have to focus on anything in particular. If you do carve out some time for unobstructed thinking, be sure to free yourself from any specific intent.

* * *

The potential of our own creativity is rapidly being compromised by the era we live in. I believe that genius in the 21st century will be attributed to people who are able to unplug from the constant state of "reactionary workflow," reduce their amount of insecurity work, and allow their minds to solve the great challenges of our era. Brilliance is so rare because it is always obstructed, often by the very stuff that keeps us so busy. ■

FREEDOM

FROM PRISON

WHEN *DOING GOOD* ISN'T REALLY *DOING GOOD*

Donald Miller

Chesterton said the idea of a sin nature is the only bit of Christian theology we can actually prove. And while there may be other bits of theology we can prove, I do agree the matter of sin nature is undeniable. That said, though, we commonly think of sin nature in remedial terms. Lying, stealing, cheating, these are all sins, while giving to charity or loving another person is not. But to classify sin so simply is to lessen the actual depravity we claim exists in man.

I'd take the idea a step further. I'd say total depravity fuels most of our good works, too. It's rare to find a successful church or ministry that isn't fueled by leadership that "needs" control or power or fame or even, sadly, the desire to be godly, which can also be wrapped up in total depravity.

The difference rests in our motives, of course. Like any addiction, self-addiction is a matter of motives and manipulation. Motives can be twisted and we can easily become deceived about why we do what we do. Do we love because we love, or do we love in order to be loved? The first is pure, the second isn't any more selfless than not loving at all. When we love in order to get security, the person we are loving is just being used, and when we act righteously to gain a sense of security in our spiritual lives, our righteousness isn't truly righteous. Maybe this is why Paul talks about his righteousness being like filthy rags. It's all a con game, and the con isn't so much on others as it is on ourselves.

Freedom from this isn't easy, and unfortunately like that old Chinese finger trap, the more we try, the worse the situation gets.

The Bible talks about doing good works without our right hand knowing what our left hand is doing. I take this to mean, among other things, we should do the good things we do from a sense of outward flowing love, a love that first requires an inward flowing love. We rarely think of controlling the sin or the self-deceptive motives in our lives as something we stop by ignoring, but this is precisely what I'm recommending.

When we meditate on how much God loves us instead of on how loving we are, we tend to love others selflessly out of a feeling of completion, while if we meditate on how much we love others in order to get them to love us back, we love others out of a sense of compulsion or need. The same is true for our righteous-

WHEN WE THINK ABOUT HOW GOOD WE ARE, WE MAY NO LONGER BE GOOD. INSTEAD, WE CAN THINK ABOUT HOW GOOD GOD IS, AND HOW MUCH WE ARE LOVED BY HIM, AND THEN JUST LIVE IN THE OVERFLOW OF THOSE TRUTHS. **IT'S TRICKY, BUT ONE IS A PRISON AND THE OTHER IS FREEDOM.**

ness. When we think about how good we are, we may no longer be good. Instead, we can think about how good God is, and how much we are loved by Him, and then just live in the overflow of those truths. It's tricky, but one is a prison and the other is freedom.

The good news is that our motives don't really matter in the eternal scheme of things, at least not to us personally. As people who are one with Christ, God sees in us his Son, and the righteousness of his Son is the reason he interacts with us. So in loving others, we can be agents of God, loving others for God, through ourselves, rather than loving others for ourselves and through ourselves. It all sounds like mind gymnastics, but it doesn't have to be that hard. The best thing I can do to love my friends is to think about and live within the truth that God loves me. This is the only way I can live and love without expecting a return on my investment. The real love will happen naturally once I understand my need is met. I don't have to think about my motives at all. **C**

Originally appeared at donmilleris.com and is used by permission.

REFLECTION

One of the primary ways our community can engage in culture is by participating in God's "grand restoration project" —actively conspiring with God in the redemption of all things. God is at work all around us and it is our charge to understand our context and be present to the needs He has put directly in front of us.

Our generation has made great strides in engaging culture by investing in the kingdom initiatives of bringing hope, justice, and peace to our communities. But what is our motivation? Is it mere coincidence that an increased awareness and participation in justice issues within the church coincides with an increased awareness of justice issues within popular culture? Is the church influencing the culture or being influenced by the culture? Is it possible that our motivations for justice are more rooted in raising our cool quotient rather than showing the love of Christ to a lost and hurting world?

Here, Donald Miller gives us a tremendous reminder of own depravity. He reminds us that we are incapable of doing good in and of ourselves. He shows us that any "true good" that comes from us is an outflow of the Spirit within us. So does this mean that we shouldn't participate in social initiatives unless we know our motives are pure? Not at all! If we waited until our motives were pure to participate in life we would never move forward in anything. But it is helpful to gauge our motivations in doing good, so here are a few things to consider:

1
MAKE GOD'S LOVE FOR YOU YOUR FOUNDATION

First John 4:19 tells us that we love because He first loved us. God's love and grace for us must be the foundation and motivation of every good work we do. As Don tells us, our love for others must be the outflowing of God's love for us.

2
MEDITATE ON GOD'S WORD

Having God's love for us as our ultimate motivation is easier said than done. Often we say we understand God's love for us but our insecure actions tell a different story. Paul gives us a clue in Romans 12 of how to change our motivations when he tells us that we are transformed by the renewing of our mind. If we meditate on the truth of God's Word, the voice of His truth will become louder than the voice of our circumstances and emotions.

3
ACT IN OBEDIENCE

C.S. Lewis tells us that "to know God is to know that our obedience is due to Him." Sometimes our best course of action is to just move forward in obedience even when our motives are not pure. Often it is the action that will end up changing our motivation.

WHAT IS PLACE?

Craig Bartholomew

Place is ubiquitous and yet always particular. Place is my backyard in Hamilton, Ontario, Canada, where the spring bulbs are now flowering and where a wild rabbit comes for a time to rest and graze, at peace amidst this busy city. Place is my office, painted a warm yellow by friends when I moved in here and where I sit to write this book. Place is the unutterable beauty of the Valley of a Thousand Hills, near where I grew up in KwaZulu-Natal in South Africa, the same context in which Alan Paton's classic novel, *Cry, the Beloved Country*,[1] is set.

Cry, the Beloved Country poured out of Paton while he was on a trip to Europe in 1946. Having just arrived in Norway and after visiting a cathedral, filled with intense homesickness, he returned to his hotel room, where he wrote the opening lines of what was to become a classic: "There is a lovely road that runs from Ixopo into the hills. These hills are grass-covered and rolling, and they are lovely beyond any singing of it."[2] That same beloved country is the scene of Nobel Prize-winning author J. M. Coetzee's *Disgrace*, with its almost unreadable accounts of rape and violence in post-apartheid South Africa.

Place is the rich, African beauty of Rwanda and churches filled with human skulls from the genocide that still—how long?—indelibly marks the landscape of that country. Place is an Amish farm, and the animal factory, "which, like the concentration camp, is a vision of Hell."[3] Place is the home one retreats to for rest and nourishment, and place is the "homes" that are the scene of abuse. Place is Mother Teresa's home for the dying in Calcutta—"something beautiful for God"—with its translucent light caught on camera by Malcolm Muggeridge, and also Birkenau and Auschwitz. Place is gardens and parks, and millions of kilometers of road and millions of square acres of tarred parking lots. Place is my house, my garden, the university at which I teach, the city in which I live, the malls in which I shop, and the roads and trails on which I run.

* * *

Place is a rich, thick[4] concept which is notoriously difficult to define. As Aristotle rightly noted, "The question, what is place? presents many difficulties."[5] Place is real, but it is a complex creational structure. Place is so fundamental to human existence and so ubiquitous that, paradoxically, it is easy to miss.[6] Its reality and importance cannot be in doubt, but the neglect of it and its thickness make it hard to pin down conceptually.

Firstly, place is a quintessentially *human* concept in that it is part of our creatureliness. E. Casey, who has done the most comprehensive work on the philosophy of place, notes that "to be in the world, to be situated at all, is to be in place. Place is the phenomenal particularization of 'being-in-the-world,' a phrase that in Heidegger's hands retains a certain formality and abstractness which only the concreteness of *being-in-place*, that is, being in the *place-world* itself, can mitigate."[7] Casey speaks in this respect of the human condition as one of *implacement*: "To exist at all . . . is to have a place—*to be implaced*, however minimally or temporarily."[8] Part of being embodied involves being in a particular place: "In my embodied being I am *just at* a place as its inner boundary; a surrounding landscape, on the other hand, is *just beyond* that place as its outer boundary. Between the two boundaries—and very much as a function of their different interplay—implacement occurs. Place is what takes place between body and landscape."[9]

Secondly, since to be human is to be placed, it follows that place results from the *dynamic interaction* of humans and their particular locations. While human existence in the world is possible only in and through a particular place, place is also shaped and constituted by the activity of the humans who dwell in it. The interplay between humans and their contexts means that place has a developmental, *cultural* dimension.[10] Place is furthermore never individualistic; rather, it "insinuates itself into a collectivity."[11] There is inevitably a *social* dimension to place; humans are placed in relationship, and in relationship they form and fashion places. Implacement is an ongoing, dynamic process, and, being cultural and social, it is also *historical*. These dimensions contribute "to the felt density of a particular place, the sense that it has something lasting to it."[12] An exploration of place will thus attend to dimensions such as the natural landscape, flora and fauna, patterns of weather and sky, the human shaping of a place and its resources, the history of a place, memory, and the individual and communal narratives with which a place is imbued.[13]

Thirdly, although *space* and *place* are inseparable, place must be distinguished from space. [...] Place is part of our lived, everyday experience, whereas space, especially in our modern world, is a theoretical concept and as such an abstraction *from* the lived experience of place. There has been a fatal tendency in modernity to privilege abstract, scientific knowledge over everyday experience as the path to the truth about the world. Such an approach sounds the death knell for place, since it fails to do justice to the thick, rich, holding action of local habitation.[14] Primacy must, we will argue, be given to lived, everyday experience in our knowledge of the world.

WHY DOES PLACE MATTER?

We live amidst a crisis of place. In our late-modern age we have lost that very human sense of place amidst the time-space compression[15] characteristic of "postmodernity" and globalization. Place has become something that one moves through, preferably at great speed, and virtual reality is no *replacement*. As David Lyon perceptively notes of cyberspace, "There is no place to this space."[16] Casey describes our culture as *dromocratic*, that is, as a speedbound era.[17] Indeed, the suffering of placelessness is not confined to refugees and those in exile, agonizing as their experiences are; in our dromocratic society every person constantly "on the move" suffers from placelessness in one form or another.

* * *

Place is so constituent of human beings that perhaps this is one reason why it is so easily overlooked. But we desperately need to recover a sense of place and placemaking. "The present moment is a propitious one for assessing the fate of place. This is so even though there is precious little talk of place in philosophy—or, for that matter, in psychology or sociology, literary theory or religious studies."[18] Theology and biblical studies suffer a similar neglect.[19] Emphases on an existentialist approach and a great-deeds approach resulted in the neglect of creation, nature, land, and place in most biblical theology. Brueggemann's *The Land* marked a significant reversal in this trend, and, encouragingly, an ecological biblical hermeneutic and theology are emerging with similar concerns. However, it is rare to find theologians and biblical exegetes working specifically with the concept of *place*. "Place" is particularly well suited to excavate key elements of the biblical message and to help us recover a robust practice of place today. ∎

1 The title is drawn from a phrase that is used several times in the book. For example, from p. 80: "Cry, the beloved country, for the unborn child that is the inheritor of our fear. Let him not love the earth too deeply. Let him not laugh too gladly when the water runs through his fingers, nor stand too silent when the setting sun makes red the veld with fire. Let him not be too moved when the birds of his land are singing, nor give too much of his heart to a mountain or a valley. For fear will rob him of all if he gives too much."

2 See Paton, *Towards the Mountain*, 264–74.

3 W. Berry, *Way of Ignorance*, 99.

4 In Geertz's sense of the term as found in *Interpretation of Cultures*, 5–6, 9–10.

5 Aristotle, *Physics* 4.1.34.

6 Cf. Malpas, *Place and Experience*, 177–78.

7 Casey, *Getting Back into Place*, xv. Emphasis original. Casey notes that "Heidegger alone of postmodern thinkers has thematized place, albeit fragmentarily and inconsistently" (*Fate of Place*, 11). It is therefore not surprising that Casey uses Heidegger's terminology in defining place.

8 Ibid., 13. Emphasis original.

9 Ibid., 29. Emphasis original.

10 Ibid.

11 Ibid., 31.

12 Ibid., 33.

13 Malpas, *Place and Experience*, 185.

14 Casey, *Fate of Place*, 20.

15 See Harvey, *Condition of Postmodernity*, 260–83, on this theme.

16 Lyon, *Jesus in Disneyland*, 124. Cf. Casey, *Fate of Places*, xiv; and Ware, *Cities of God*, 245.

17 Casey, *Getting Back into Place*, xiv.

18 Casey, *Fate of Place*, xi–xii.

19 Inge, *Christian Theology of Place*, is an important exception.

WISDOM

&

SABBATH REST

—

Dr. Timothy Keller

7

13

AR

14

9

1

2

10

15

11

3

16

11

12

4

17

12

5

13

18

13

14

5

14

7

15

6

19

14

15

8

7

20

15

16

9

8

21

16

17

16

9

22

17

18

10

17

18

10

23

19

18

11

19

11

20

24

12

12

20

25

13

13

21

26

14

22

Leadership is stewardship—the cultivation of the resources God has entrusted to us for his glory. The Sabbath gives us both theological and practical help in managing one of our primary resources—our time.

In Ephesians 5, Paul invokes the biblical concept of wisdom:

> *"Be very careful, then, how you live—not as unwise but as wise, making the most of every opportunity, because the days are evil. Therefore do not be foolish, but understand what the Lord's will is."*
> (Ephesians 5:15–17 NIV).

The King James Version translates verses 15–16 as, "walk circumspectly, not as fools, but as wise, redeeming the time, because the days are evil." Living wisely (or circumspectly) is to a great degree a matter of how we spend our time.

So what does this verse tell us? First, the word *redeem* is drawn from the commercial marketplace. It means, essentially, to "make a killing" in the market, or to spend so wisely and strategically that the returns are many times that of the investment.

Second, Paul's phrase "the days are evil" doesn't simply mean his readers were living in bad times. When Paul speaks of "the present evil age" (Galatians 1:4), he means the time between the first coming and the second coming of Christ. It's the overlap between the old age and the new kingdom age, a time when Christians are spreading the gospel and being a witness to the kingdom. Thus, Christians are solemnly obliged not to waste time. Time-stewardship is a command!

However, applying the principle of "making the most of every opportunity" from a kingdom perspective may be harder today than ever. Especially in global cities, we find more pressure, fewer boundaries, and less stability in our daily work than perhaps ever before. Part of the issue is how connected we are through technology. Part of it is globalization, which creates such enormous economic pressures that everybody is pushed to their limits. Employers are trying to get so much productivity out of workers that many of us are being asked to go beyond what is really fair and right.

Even though technology and contemporary idols have created longer and longer work weeks, "do not be foolish, but understand what the Lord's will is." Discern God's will. Long ago someone told me that God does not give you more to do in a day than you can actually do, and I've wrestled with that for many years. We may feel there's way too much to do, but some of it is not his will. The pressure is coming from you, or your employer, or your friends, or your parents, or someone else besides God!

One of the fundamental principles of the Bible when it comes to time management is the Sabbath. If we are to be an "alternate city" (Matthew 5:14–16), we have to be different from our neighbors in how we spend our time outside of work; that is, how we rest. So what is the Sabbath about?

According to the Bible, it is about more than just taking time off. After creating the world, God looked around and saw that "it was very good" (Genesis 1:31). God did not just cease from his labor; he stopped and enjoyed what he had made. What does this mean for us? We need to stop to enjoy God, to enjoy his creation, to enjoy the fruits of our labor. The whole point of Sabbath is joy in what God has done.

Writer Judith Shulevitz describes the dynamic of work and Sabbath rest this way:

My mood would darken until, by Saturday afternoon, I'd be unresponsive and morose. My normal routine, which involved brunch with friends and swapping tales of misadventure in the relentless quest for romance and professional success, made me feel impossibly restless. I started spending Saturdays by myself. After a while I got lonely and did something that, as a teenager profoundly put off by her religious education, I could never have imagined wanting to do. I began dropping in on a nearby synagogue.

It was only much later that I developed a theory about my condition. I was suffering from the lack [of a Sabbath]. There is ample evidence that our relationship to work is out of whack. Ours is a society that pegs status to overachievement; we can't help admiring workaholics. Let me argue, instead, on behalf of an institution that has kept workaholism in reasonable check for thousands of years.

Most people mistakenly believe that all you have to do to stop working is not work. The inventors of the Sabbath understood that it was a much more complicated undertaking. You cannot downshift casually and easily. This is why the Puritan and Jewish Sabbaths were so exactingly intentional. The rules did not exist to torture the faithful. They were meant to communicate the insight that interrupting the ceaseless round of striving requires a surprisingly strenuous act of will, one that has to be bolstered by habit as well as by social sanction.[1]

In the Bible, Sabbath rest means to cease regularly from and to enjoy the results of your work. It provides balance: "Six days you shall labor and do all your work, but the seventh day is a Sabbath to the Lord your God" (Exodus 20:9–10 NIV). Although Sabbath rest receives a much smaller amount of time than work, it is a necessary counterbalance so that the rest of your work can be good and beneficial.

God liberated his people when they were slaves in Egypt, and in Deuteronomy 5:12–15, God ties the Sabbath to freedom from slavery. Anyone who overworks is really a slave. Anyone who cannot rest from work is a slave—

JAN   2   3   4   5   6   7   8

6   7   8   9   10   11   12   13   14

4   5   3   4   5   6   7   8   9   MAR   1

2   3   2   3   4   5   6   7   9   10   2

FEB   1   APR   1   MAY   1   2   1

4   5   6   7   8   9   3

2   3   4   5   6   7   8   9   10   11   4

JUNE   1   2   3   4   5   AUG   1   2   10   11   12

2   3   SEPT   1   2   3   4   11   12   13

OCT   1   2   3   4   5   5   6

JULY   1   1   2   3   4   5   6   6   7

NOV   1   2   3   4   5   6   7   7   8

DEC   1   2   3   8   9

9

31

31

30   31

30   30

29

31   29   29   28   30

30   28

28   28   14

to a need for success, to a materialistic culture, to exploitative employers, to parental expectations, or to all of the above. These slave masters will abuse you if you are not disciplined in the practice of Sabbath rest. Sabbath is a declaration of freedom.

Thus Sabbath is about more than external rest of the body; it is about inner rest of the soul. We need rest from the anxiety and strain of our overwork, which is really an attempt to justify ourselves—to gain the money or the status or the reputation we think we have to have. Avoiding overwork requires deep rest in Christ's finished work for your salvation (Hebrews 4:1–10). Only then will you be able to "walk away" regularly from your vocational work and rest.

Sabbath is the key to getting this balance, and Jesus identifies himself as the Lord of the Sabbath (Mark 2:27–28)—the Lord of Rest! Jesus urges us, "Come to me, all you who are weary and burdened, and I will give you rest. Take my yoke upon you and learn from me, for I am gentle and humble in heart, and you will find rest for your souls" (Matthew 11:28–29). One of the great blessings of the gospel is that he gives you rest that no one else will.

SABBATH "PRACTICALS"

In practical terms, how do we figure out how much time we need for Sabbath rest, and how do we spend that time? The following are a few suggestions or guidelines, by no means exhaustive.

What is the ideal amount of time off from work?

The Ten Commandments require one day (twenty-four hours) off each week. When God gave these commandments, the Hebrews had been working from sunup to sundown, but the gift of the Sabbath was to stop working at sundown on Friday and rest until sundown on Saturday.

If you look at the Scripture, there's nothing that says you have to confine yourself to a forty- or fifty-hour work week. I suggest that to be within the biblical boundaries, you need to have at least one full day off, and the equivalent of an additional half-day off during the week.

For example, if your work and commute take up almost all of your weekdays but you have a full weekend off, with church participation on Sundays, then that is probably a sufficient Sabbath. Or if you get one full day off per week, and perhaps three evenings free after 6:00 p.m, you can live a pretty balanced life. This still allows quite a lot of hours for work during the week.

What counts as time off?

Of course, "making the most of every opportunity" is not simple. It never has been simple. Yes, two hours spent in prayer with God will produce far more spiritual benefits than watching an old Cary Grant movie; yet, recreation is something you must have! Mental refreshment is part of a balanced diet for the body and soul, so prayer cannot replace all recreation, exercise, and so on. Sabbath encompasses several different types of rest, as outlined below.

1. TAKE SOME TIME FOR SHEER INACTIVITY.

Most people need some time every week that is unplanned and unstructured, in which you can do whatever you feel like doing. If your Sabbath time is very busy and filled with scheduled activities of "recreation" and ministry, it will not suffice. There must be some cessation from activity or exertion. This pause in the work cycle is analogous to Israel's practice of letting a field lie fallow every seventh year to produce whatever happened to grow (Leviticus 25:1–7). The soil rested so over-farming would not deplete its nutrients and destroy its ability to keep producing. Whatever came up in the soil came up. You need some unscheduled time like that every week to let come up—out of the heart and mind—whatever will.

2. TAKE SOME TIME FOR AVOCATIONAL ACTIVITY.

An avocation is something that is sheer pleasure to you, but that does require some intentionality and gives some structure to your Sabbath rest. In many cases an avocation is something that others do for "work," which is analogous to occasionally planting a different crop in a field to replenish the nutrients and make the soil more fertile for its normal crop. Include these elements:

» You need some contemplative rest. Prayer and worship are a critical part of Sabbath rest, from any perspective. Regular time for devotion, reading the Scripture, and listening to God forms the basis for inner rest and provides time away from the more exhausting exertions of life.

» You need some recreational rest. The Puritans and others were rightly skeptical of recreations that required spending a great deal of money and time and exertion, because those types of recreations exhaust people. Be careful that recreation really refreshes.

» You need to include aesthetic rest. Expose yourself to works of God's creation that refresh and energize you, and that you find beautiful. This may mean outdoor things. It may mean art—music, drama, and visual art. God looked around at the world he made and said it was good, so aesthetic rest is necessary for participating in God's Sabbath fully.

3. CONSIDER WHETHER YOU ARE AN INTROVERT OR AN EXTROVERT.

When planning your Sabbath rest, ask yourself what really "recharges" you. This self-assessment can help you determine how relational your Sabbath time should be. Introverts tend to spend their energy when out with people and recharge their batteries by being alone. Extroverts tend to spend energy in personal work and recharge their batteries by getting out with people. If you are a real introvert, be careful about trying to maintain all of your community-building relationships during your Sabbath time. That would be too draining. On the other hand, relationship-building could be one of the greatest things a true extrovert could possibly do. Don't try to imitate an introvert's Sabbath rhythms if you are an extrovert or vice versa! Recognize that some avocational activities take you into solitude, while some take you out into society.

4. DON'T NECESSARILY COUNT FAMILY TIME AS SABBATH TIME.

Do a realistic self-assessment of "family time" and how it affects you. Family time is important, but parents need to be very careful that they don't let all of their regular Sabbath time be taken up with parental responsibilities. (Introverts especially will need time away from the kids!) Keeping all of these things in good balance may be virtually impossible when your children are very young, but this too will pass.

5. HONOR BOTH MICRO-AND MACRO-RHYTHMS IN YOUR SEASONS OF REST.

Israel's Sabbath cycles of rest-and-work included not only Sabbath days but also Sabbath years and even a Year of Jubilee every forty-nine years (Leviticus 25:8–11). This is a crucial insight for workers in today's world. It is possible to voluntarily take on a season of work that requires high energy, long hours, and insufficient weekly Sabbath time. A new physician has to work long hours in a residency program, for example, and many other careers (such as finance, government, and law) similarly demand some sort of initial period of heavy, intense work. Starting your own business or pursuing a major project like making a movie will require something similar. In these situations you have to watch that you don't justify too little Sabbath by saying you're "going through a season"—when in actual fact that season never ends.

If you must enter a season like this, it should not last longer than two or three years at the most. Be accountable to someone for this, or you will get locked into an "under-Sabbathed" lifestyle, and you will burn out. And during this "under-Sabbathed" time, do not let the rhythms of prayer, Bible study, and worship die. Be creative, but get it in.

BRAINSTORM IDEAS WITH OTHERS

As soon as Christian communities start defining specific rules for what everyone can and can't do on the Sabbath (like traveling, watching television, or recreation, for example), we begin to slip into legalism. Observing Sabbath rest along with a community can be beneficial, but keep in mind that people differ widely in their temperaments and situations.

It may be helpful to find other Christians in your field of work and ask them how they handle the need for rest, leisure, and restoration. Inquire about their weekly or seasonal rhythms. You will probably discover one or two ideas that are really helpful. If you can, bring these people together to brainstorm in person.

We live in a broken world, and some employers do relentlessly exploit their employees. Dealing with situations like these is difficult, but being part of a community made up of wise Christians in your field can help you correctly assess your work situation and your alternatives.

"INJECTING" SABBATH INTO OUR WORK LIVES

I have come to see that if you develop the foundation and inner rest of Sabbath, it will not simply make you more disciplined about taking time off, but it will also lead you to be less frantic and driven in your work itself. This is perhaps the most important application of Sabbath, where we can truly act as a counterculture, and here's how it works.

Associated with the Sabbath laws were "gleaning laws," such as Leviticus 19:9, in which field owners were not allowed to "reap to the very edges" of their fields. They had to leave a percentage of grain in the field for the poor to come and harvest. Sabbath, then, is the deliberate limitation of productivity, as a way to trust God, be a good steward of your self, and declare freedom from slavery to our work.

In concrete terms this is the hardest thing to do, because it's a heart matter. Personally, this has meant deliberately setting fewer goals for myself in a given day and week, rather than harvesting "out to the edges." In global cities, many people are stingy with their money yet freely give their bodies away.

By contrast, we Christians are stingy with our bodies and generous with our money. Likewise, many people are willing to mortgage their souls to work, but at a certain point Christians have to say, "I'm willing to set fewer goals, not go up the ladder as fast, and even risk not accomplishing as much, because I have to take Sabbath time off. And ultimately, I don't need to be incredibly successful. I can choose this path of freedom because of the inner rest I've received from Jesus Christ through what he has done for me."

You have to actually inject this Sabbath rest into your thinking and into your work life. Some of our work worlds are institutionally structured toward overwork. Sometimes you have to "pay your dues" in the early stages of your career when you're in a season of hard work (as I mentioned previously) or are trying to gain some credibility in your field. When you're more established in your field, you may be able to moderate your workload. However, at some point, even if that doesn't happen, you will have to trust God and honor Jesus—who is Lord of the Sabbath—by practicing Sabbath and risk "falling behind" in your career.

It may happen that you will fall behind, and yet retain your sanity. Or it may be that God will allow you to keep moving ahead in your career despite your practice of Sabbath and the "gleaning" principle. It is up to him.

CONCLUSION

The purpose of Sabbath is not simply to rejuvenate yourself in order to do more production, nor is it the pursuit of pleasure. The purpose of Sabbath is to enjoy your God, life in general, what you have accomplished in the world through his help, and the freedom you have in the gospel—the freedom from slavery to any material object or human expectation. The Sabbath is a sign of the hope that we have in the world to come. ⏹

---

[1]Paraphrase of Judith Shulevitz, "Bring Back the Sabbath," *The New York Times Magazine*, March 2, 2003.

REFLECTION

How you manage your time matters. Just like your money, if you squander it you'll be left scratching your head wondering what happened to it and why you didn't accomplish more with what you had been given. Dr. Keller presents the leader with a practical guide to stewarding our time regarding Sabbath rest. But it's up to you to make sure your team understands these principles.

It's not enough to schedule a couple of meetings to discuss this article. The most effective way to instill these principles into your team is to model them. You are accountable for their well-being in terms of vocational effectiveness and overall spiritual health. In order to influence those you seek to lead, it's paramount that you focus on the principles in this article and make them yours.

So, how can you influence without opening your mouth and preaching at them or calling another meeting? Here are a few ideas to get you started.

1
INFLUENCE IS NOT THE GOAL, IT'S THE BY-PRODUCT

Don't get caught up trying to influence your team. Rather, bear down on what it means for you to lead out in the area of Sabbath rest. Get serious about your commitment of keeping Sabbath a time of rest and rejuvenation. Spend time developing it as a habit.

2
DON'T TALK ABOUT IT, DO IT

Instead of calling a meeting to discuss Sabbath rest, schedule a Sabbath rest for your team. Imagine the ripples this would send to the ranks when they discover that you value their spiritual formation. Perhaps it's a day at the local monastery or weekend retreat to a secluded cabin. If your team experiences the Sabbath element at work, they're more apt to begin including it in their own private life.

3
PLAN FOR MINIMAL STRUCTURE

Dr. Keller suggests that we plan fewer goals; in essence we plan to achieve less. This allows for margin in our personal lives. Establishing a work environment that does not focus primarily on goal setting and achieving will infuse your team with a sense of confidence. No one enjoys a work environment driven by fear and anxiety. Make it your priority to set the expectations for the team. Take a risk and do fewer "things." Practice being together more and watch that seep into your congregation.

FOR REFRESHMENT AND PEACE

O God, in the course of this busy life, give us times of refreshment and peace; and grant that we may so use our leisure to rebuild our bodies and renew our minds, that our spirits may be opened to the goodness of your creation; through Jesus Christ our Lord. *Amen.* (BCP)

CONTRIBUTORS

CRAIG G. BARTHOLOMEW (PhD, University of Bristol) is professor of philosophy, religion, and theology at Redeemer University College in Ancaster, Ontario, where he holds the H. Evan Runner Chair. He is the author of *Ecclesiastes in the Baker Commentary on the Old Testament Wisdom and Psalms series*, an associate editor of Dictionary for Theological Interpretation of the Bible, and the coauthor, with Michael W. Goheen, of *The Drama of Scripture* and *Living at the Crossroads*.

MARK BATTERSON serves as lead pastor of National Community Church (www.theaterchurch.com) in Washington DC. Targeting emerging generations, 73 percent of NCCers are single twenty-somethings that live or work on Capitol Hill. Currently one church with three locations, the vision of NCC is to meet in movie theaters @ metro stops throughout the DC area. The theaterchurch.com podcast is one of the fastest-growing church podcasts in America. Mark is also a daily blogger @ www.markbatterson.com. Mark lives on Capitol Hill with his wife, Lora, and three children.

SCOTT BELSKY has committed his professional life to help organize creative individuals, teams, and networks. He is the author of the national best-selling book, *Making Ideas Happen,* and is the founder and CEO of Behance, a company that develops products and services for the creative industries. Behance's products include the Behance Network, the world's leading platform for creative professionals; The 99%, Behance's think tank for leadership and execution in creative industries, and Action Method, a popular online/mobile productivity application and line of organizational paper products. In 2010, Scott was included in *Fast Company's* list of "100 Most Creative People in Business." He attended Cornell University as an undergraduate and received his MBA from Harvard Business School.

CHRISTINE CAINE is a sought-after speaker around the world, and is passionate about the God life and seeing the local church flourish across the earth. She is a gifted communicator with a heart for reaching the lost and helping people unlock their God-given potential. She is one of the pastors and directors of Equip & Empower Ministries, as well as the founder of the A21 Campaign. Together with her husband, Nick, and daughters Catherine and Sophia, Christine spends much of the year traveling to reach the lost, strengthen leadership, champion the cause of justice, and build the local church globally. She is the author of *A Life Unleashed*, *The Core Issue*, *Run To Win* and *Can I Have (and do) It All, Please?*

MATT CHANDLER serves as lead pastor of The Village Church in Highland Village, TX. He describes his eight-year tenure at The Village as a re-planting effort where he was involved in changing the theological and philosophical culture of the congregation. The church has witnessed a tremendous response growing from 160 people to over 8,000 including satellite campuses in Dallas and Denton. Alongside his current role as lead pastor, Matt is involved in church planting efforts both locally and internationally through The Village and various strategic partnerships. His greatest joy outside of Jesus is being married to Lauren and being a dad to their three children, Audrey, Reid, and Norah.

TIM CHESTER is a director of the Porterbrook Institute which provides affordable, Bible-college level training for church leadership and missional church in the context of your ministry (www.porterbrookinstitute.org). He is a leader of The Crowded House, a church planting network (www.thecrowdedhouse.org). He blogs at www.timchester.co.uk. He is the author of a number of books and series editor of *The Good Book Guides* (The Good Book Company). He is married with two daughters.

ESTHER FLEECE is the assistant to the president for millennial relations at Focus on the Family. Fleece connects the global Christian ministry with the twenty-something generation, ensuring this influential demographic is aware of the myriad ways Focus helps families thrive. She has been featured in *Mother Jones*, *Outreach*, and *Christianity Today*, and has spoken to the National Day of Prayer Summit, the National Conference on Christian Apologetics, and the Religion Newswriters Association.

PHILEENA HEUERTZ is a spiritual director with Word Made Flesh based in Omaha, Nebraska. She is the author of the recent book *Pilgrimage of a Soul* (InterVarsity Press).

TIMOTHY KELLER is the pastor of Redeemer Presbyterian Church in Manhattan, which he started in 1989 with his wife, Kathy, and three young sons. Today, Redeemer has nearly six thousand regular attendees at five services, a host of daughter churches, and is planting churches in large cities throughout the world. He is the *New York Times* bestselling author of *The Reason for God*, *The Prodigal God*, and *Counterfeit Gods*.

JOHN MACMURRAY has a master's degree from Western Seminary and has taught the Bible for nearly thirty years. For over two decades he has made his living as a landscape nature photographer. John lives in the Pacific Northwest with his wife, Terri, and their three children, Chris, Elle, and Cassy.

BRITT MERRICK is an author, a speaker, and the lead pastor of Reality Carpinteria. He grew up entrenched in the surf industry, working for his parents' business, Channel Islands Surfboards. In the fall of 2003, sensing a further call to ministry, Britt laid Channel Island Surfboards aside and he and his wife, along with some close friends, started a church called Reality in his hometown of Carpinteria. Since then, the Reality family has grown to include churches in Ventura, Los Angeles, Stockton, San Francisco, and London. Britt lives with his wife, Kate, and their two children in Carpinteria.

JONATHAN MERRITT is a faith and culture writer who has been published in outlets such as *USA Today*, *BeliefNet*, and *Christianity Today*. He is author of *Green Like God: Unlocking the Divine Plan for Our Planet* (FaithWords, 2010) and teaching pastor at Cross Pointe Church.

DONALD MILLER is the author of multiple *New York Times* bestsellers including *Blue Like Jazz* and *A Million Miles in a Thousand Years*. He has served on the Presidential Task Force on Fatherhood and Healthy Families and is a sought-after speaker regarding narrative structure as it relates to a person's life and their projects. Don recently launched the Storyline Conference that helps people structure their lives using a cohesive narrative. He is the founder of The Mentoring Project and blogs almost daily at www.donmilleris.com

DAVID PLATT is an American pastor. He is currently the head pastor of The Church at Brook Hills in Birmingham, AL, and he is also the author of the *New York Times* bestseller *Radical: Taking Back Your Faith from the American Dream*. Platt released his follow-up book, *Radical Together: Unleashing the People of God for the Purpose of God* in April, 2011.

JUDAH AND CHELSEA SMITH are the lead pastors of The City Church in Seattle, Washington. They were the pastors of Generation Church, the youth ministry of The City Church, for ten years before stepping into their new role in 2009. Judah is the author of several books, including *Dating Delilah*, a book on purity from a new perspective. He also ministers nationally and internationally at churches and conferences, imparting into the lives of Christian leaders and young people. His ministry is noted for an anointed, fresh preaching style mixed with humor, authority, passion, and strong faith.

ANDY STANLEY is a pastor, communicator, author, and the founder of North Point Ministries (NPM). Since its inception in 1995, North Point Ministries has grown from one campus to three in the Atlanta area and has helped plant over twenty strategic partner churches throughout the United States. Each Sunday, more than twenty thousand adults attend worship services at one of NPM's three campuses: North Point Community Church, Browns Bridge Community Church, and Buckhead Church. Andy's books include the newly released *The Grace of God*, as well as *Communicating for a Change*, *Making Vision Stick*, *Next Generation Leader*, *The Principle of the Path*, and *How Good is Good Enough?* Andy lives in Alpharetta, GA with his wife, Sandra, and their three children.

JUD WILHITE is an author, a speaker, and the senior pastor of Central Christian Church, Las Vegas. More than nineteen thousand people attend its multiple campuses each weekend. Jud's books include *Throw It Down*, *Eyes Wide Open*, and *Uncensored Grace*. Jud and his wife, Lori, reside in the Las Vegas area with their children and a slobbery bulldog named Roxy.

TIMOTHY WILLARD AND JASON LOCY are the co-authors of *Veneer: Living Deeply In A Surface Society* (Zondervan, 2011). Timothy is an Atlanta-based writer who holds a master of arts in religion. Jason is the creative director of FiveStone, an award-winning multidisciplinary design studio located in historic Buford, GA.

BE PRESENT

CONTRIBUTORS:

Craig Bartholomew	Tim Chester	John MacMurray	Judah Smith
Mark Batterson	Esther Fleece	Britt Merrick	Andy Stanley
Scott Belsky	Phileena Heuertz	Jonathan Merritt	Jud Wilhite
Christine Caine	Jason Locy	Donald Miller	Timothy Willard
Matt Chandler	Timothy Keller	David Platt	

UTILIZING THIS REVIEW: We designed this year's volume for both individual and group study. Throughout the publication you will find "Reflection" pages that provide you with study prompts and discussion questions. We also encourage you to bring your own questions to the group and explore these ideas together. Conversation is a starting point for community, and the group will grow through your dialogue. Challenge each person to bring a question, a new thought, or a conviction to wrestle with each time you meet. You'll also notice several pages containing prayers and/or Scripture. Do not skim these page. Use them to actually pray and meditate on God's Word and what he is teaching you through the articles.

A CATALYST LEADER IS:
Intentional About Community
Engaged in Culture
Uncompromising in Integrity
Passionate About God
Courageous in Calling
Authentic in Influence

Printed in the United States of America.
Copyright ©2011 by Catalyst

ISBN: 978-0-9832118-7-7

All book excerpts and articles used by permission.

Editor:
Tim Willard

Contributing Editor:
Jason Haynes

Creative Direction and Design:

FiveStone, Buford, Georgia
www.fivestone.com.

SPECIAL THANKS TO:

Christine, Lyric and Brielle Willard, Jason Locy, Brad Lomenick, Donna Pennell, Jason Haynes, Craig Canfield, Pato Juarez, Teresa Cunningham, Ken Coleman, Joshua Garrels, Bilbo Baggins, Flynn Rider, and all our contributors.

For more information on the Catalyst Conference or to order additional copies of *Be Present: Where You Are* call 888.334.6569 or visit **catalystspace.com**.

HERE TO SERVE
(church leaders like you)

You're our priority. That's why Zondervan is partnering with today's most trusted Christian leaders and ministry practitioners to create tools that support your ministry. Our continued commitment is to develop innovative resources—like the NIV, small group curriculum, books, and preaching and teaching resources—that help you lead your congregation into a deeper relationship with God and each other.

WHAT WOULD FEED A MOUSE WOULD STARVE AN ELEPHANT.

GOD NEVER GROWS TWO PEOPLE THE SAME WAY.
-John Ortberg

We are all unique and so is your spiritual life.
Monvee's "one of a kind" online spiritual assessment can help you discover your
unique wiring and then help you grow in a way that fits you.

To see all that Monvee has to offer, check out www.monvee.com today!

HOW CAN WE CHERISH THE FAITH OF
OUR PARENTS WHILE ALSO TAKING HOLD
OF IT OURSELVES?

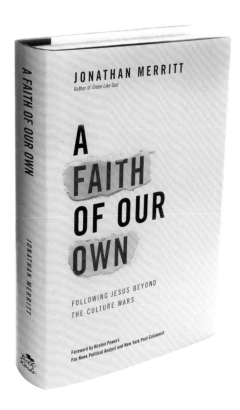

A FAITH OF OUR OWN

FOLLOWING JESUS BEYOND THE CULTURE WARS

Faith
Words

TABLE OF CONTENTS

A FRANCISCAN BENEDICTION